Best Storage SOLUTIONS

Tips, ideas, and projects to organize your

Reader's Digest

The Reader's Digest Association, Inc.
Pleasantville, New York/Montreal

A READER'S DIGEST BOOK

FOR THE FAMILY HANDYMAN

Executive Editor	**SPIKE CARLSEN**
Special Projects Editor	**MARY FLANAGAN**
Design Director	**SARA KOEHLER**
Administrative Manager	**ALICE GARRETT**
Graphic Designer	**TERESA MARRONE**

FOR READER'S DIGEST

Vice President, General Manager, North American Publishing Group	**BONNIE BACHAR**
General Manager Home and Garden Group	**TOM OTT**
Director of Integrated Sales and Marketing	**KERRY BIANCHI**
Associate Publisher	**RICK STRAFACE**
Production	**BRIAN SCHWARZE**
Associate Art Director	**GEORGE MCKEON**
Executive Editor, Trade Publishing	**DOLORES YORK**
Manufacturing Manager	**JOHN L. CASSIDY**
Director of Production	**MICHAEL BRAUNSCHWEIGER**
Associate Publisher	**ROSANNE MCMANUS**
President and Publisher, Trade Publishing	**HAROLD CLARKE**

ISBN 13: 978-0-7621-0880-0
ISBN 10: 0-7621-0880-0

Previously published as *Best Storage Solutions* 2005.

Text, photography and illustrations for *Best Storage Solutions* are based on articles previously run in **The Family Handyman** magazine and **American Woodworker** magazine (2915 Commers Dr., Suite 700, Eagan, MN 55121), www.familyhandyman.com.

For more Reader's Digest products and information, visit our website: www.rd.com (in the United States)

www.readersdigest.ca (in Canada)

Printed in China

1 3 5 7 9 10 8 6 4 2

A NOTE TO OUR READERS: All do-it-yourself activities involve a degree of risk. Skills, materials, tools and site conditions vary widely. Although the editors have made every effort to ensure accuracy, the reader remains responsible for the selection and use of tools, materials and methods. Always obey local codes and laws, follow manufacturer instructions and observe safety precautions.

Contents

SECTION 1:
utility & garage shelves

6   Rotating garage shelves
12   Plywood storage rack
16   Foldaway workshop
26   Multipurpose towers

32 afternoon projects
▾ Under-sink shelf
▾ Upside-down shelves
▾ Behind-the-stairs storage
▾ Ceiling drawers
▾ Utility shelves
▾ Mobile stacking totes
▾ Up-and-away storage

SECTION 2:
kitchen & bathroom storage

38   Roll-out pantry
41   Corner swing- and roll-out trays
44   Space-saving cabinet
48   Door-mounted spice and lid racks
50   Pull-out trash drawer
52   Toe-kick drawers
54   Roll-out kitchen trays

58 afternoon projects
▾ Open kitchen shelves
▾ Glass shelves

60 gallery of ideas

SECTION 3:
closet shelving systems

64   Modular kit closet organizer
70   Simple closet organizer
77   Handy Hints®
78   Custom-built closet organizer

87 gallery of ideas

SECTION 4:
free-standing & wall-mounted shelves

90   Traditional maple bookcase
100   Leaning tower of shelves
106   Entryway pocket screw coat locker
113   Coat and mitten rack
116   Swedish wall shelves
120   Floating shelves–hollow door

124 afternoon projects
▾ Portable bookshelf
▾ Easy-to-build display shelving
▾ Closet rod and shelf
▾ Free-form wall shelves
▾ Stud stuffer
▾ Petite shelves

SECTION 5:
built-in shelves & bookcases

130   Cherry bookcase
140   Floor-to-ceiling bookcases
151   Handy Hints®

152 gallery of ideas

SECTION 6:
offices & entertainment centers

156   Low-cost TV cabinet

165 afternoon projects
▾ Sliding bookend
▾ Portable music box
166   Family message center
174   Stackable shelves
181   Desktop file holder

182 gallery of ideas

186   RESOURCES

188   PRODUCT GUIDE
▾ 10 Storage Solutions

section

1

utility and garage shelves

Rotating garage shelves 6

Plywood storage rack 12

Foldaway workshop 16

Multipurpose towers 26

Afternoon projects

Under-sink shelf 32

Upside-down shelves 33

Behind-the-stairs storage ..33

Ceiling drawers 34

Utility shelves 34

Mobile stacking totes 35

Up-and-away storage 35

Rotating garage shelves

Easy access for all your small stuff

Set aside a Saturday to build this handy bin, and you'll clean up all those loose boxes of screws, bolts and other small stuff that clutter your garage or workshop. This bin rotates on a pair of lazy Susan rings to maximize corner space and provide quick, easy access. A stationary upper shelf secured to the wall steadies the bin so it'll spin easily and won't tip over. You can add as many shelves as you need, or leave one bay open top to bottom for storing tall things like levels and straightedges. You won't need special joints or fasteners to construct it; simple butt joints and screws hold it all together. You need only basic carpentry tools to cut and fasten the pieces.

Materials and cost

This project costs about $100. This project was constructed from one and a half 4x8 sheets of birch plywood (about $40 per sheet, $25 per half sheet). Birch plywood is easy to work with because it's smooth and flat, but you can cut your costs by about half if you use 3/4-in. CDX-grade plywood. Buy two lazy Susan rings, 12-in. round and 3-in. square diameters, from a woodworkers' store if your home center doesn't carry them. You can find all of the other materials at most home centers, including the 3-in. vinyl base we used for the shelf edging. See the Materials List, p. 8, for a complete rundown of what you'll need.

Careful cutting and layout make assembly a snap

Cut all the pieces to size from Figure B, p. 9. Accurate cuts will result in tight, clean joints. Clamp a straightedge to the plywood to guide your circular saw when making the straight cuts. Use a carbide blade with at least 36 teeth to minimize splintering.

Photo 1 shows you how to mark the circle for the plywood bottom. Substitute a narrow strip of 1/4-in.-thick wood for the compass arm if you don't have peg board. Use the bottom as a template to mark the arcs on the quarter-circle shelves (Figure B). Use a bucket to mark the arcs on the tops of the dividers.

Before assembling the pieces, lay out the shelf locations on the dividers. Make the shelves any height you want, but making them different heights in adjacent sections simplifies the screwing process.

Fasten the shelves to the two narrow dividers first (Photo 2), then set them upright and attach them to the wide center divider (Photo 3).

Drilling an access hole is the trick to mounting the lazy Susan

At first glance, attaching the 12-in. lazy Susan is a bit mysterious. The lazy Susan rotates on ball bearings with the top ring secured to the bin bottom and the bottom ring secured to the base. Securing it to the base is straightfor-

Electrical

Tapes

Auto

DR-438X
DISTRIBUTOR CAP

Stains

Spray Paint

Plants

WD-40

WATCO

MINI
Pre-St
Wood C

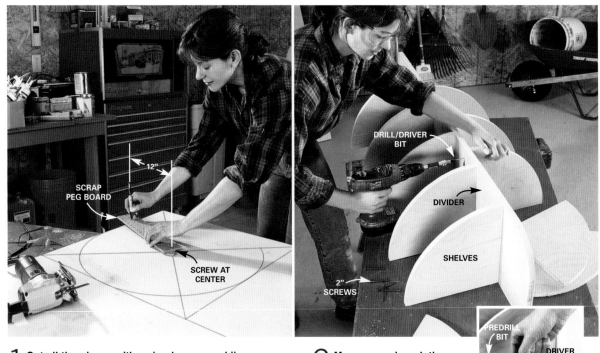

1 Cut all the pieces with a circular saw and jigsaw, using the dimensions in Figure A, p. 9, and our Cutting List. Mark the circle cut for the bottom with a 12-in. compass made from a scrap of peg board. Cut it out with a jigsaw. Then trace the arcs of the shelves using the bottom as a template. (*NOTE:* The shelf sides are 11-5/8 inches.)

2 Measure and mark the shelf locations on the dividers, spacing them anywhere from 10 to 14 in. apart. Align the shelves with these marks, then predrill and screw the shelves to the two narrow dividers with 2-in. drywall screws. A drill/driver bit speeds this process.

ward—you center it and screw it down. Once it's fastened, you have to drive screws upward to fasten the top ring to the bin bottom. The bottom ring of the lazy Susan has a special 3/4-in. access hole to help here. Drill a 3/4-in. hole in the plywood base at the access hole point (Photo 4). Then poke your screws through the access hole to fasten the top ring to the bin base (Photo 5).

The 3-in. lazy Susan rotates on square plates. You won't need an access hole to fasten them. Just screw through the holes in the corners (Photos 6 and 7).

Putting the unit in place

If you're placing the base on a concrete floor, rest it on treated 1x2s to avoid rot. Level it with shims, if needed, for smooth rotation. Fasten the support shelf to the walls (Photo 8).

materials list

- One and a half 4x8 sheets of (birch) plywood
- One 12" round lazy Susan ring
- One 3" square lazy Susan ring
- 1 lb. of 2" No. 8 screws
- Sixteen 3/4" No. 6 flat head screws
- Ten 4' strips of 3" vinyl base
- 1 lb. of 1" tacks
- One tube of vinyl base adhesive
- Two 2' treated 1x2s
- Three 2-1/2" x 3/16" masonry screws
- Eight 2-1/2" screws

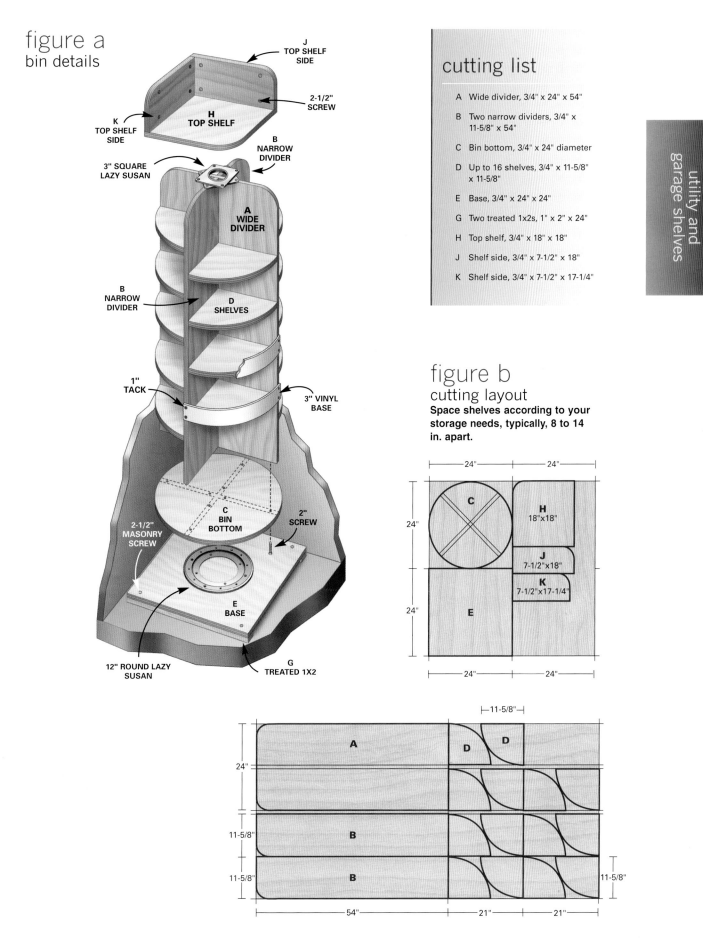

figure a
bin details

J
TOP SHELF SIDE

2-1/2" SCREW

K
TOP SHELF SIDE

H
TOP SHELF

3" SQUARE LAZY SUSAN

B
NARROW DIVIDER

A
WIDE DIVIDER

B
NARROW DIVIDER

D
SHELVES

1"
TACK

3" VINYL BASE

2-1/2"
MASONRY SCREW

C
BIN BOTTOM

2"
SCREW

E
BASE

12" ROUND LAZY SUSAN

G
TREATED 1X2

cutting list

A   Wide divider, 3/4" x 24" x 54"

B   Two narrow dividers, 3/4" x 11-5/8" x 54"

C   Bin bottom, 3/4" x 24" diameter

D   Up to 16 shelves, 3/4" x 11-5/8" x 11-5/8"

E   Base, 3/4" x 24" x 24"

G   Two treated 1x2s, 1" x 2" x 24"

H   Top shelf, 3/4" x 18" x 18"

J   Shelf side, 3/4" x 7-1/2" x 18"

K   Shelf side, 3/4" x 7-1/2" x 17-1/4"

utility and garage shelves

figure b
cutting layout
Space shelves according to your storage needs, typically, 8 to 14 in. apart.

24"   24"

24"

C

H
18"x18"

J
7-1/2"x18"

24"

E

K
7-1/2"x17-1/4"

24"   24"

11-5/8"

A

D   D

24"

B

11-5/8"

B

11-5/8"

11-5/8"

54"   21"   21"

3 Connect the two shelf assemblies to the wide center divider with 2-in. drywall screws. Center and screw the circular bottom to the dividers.

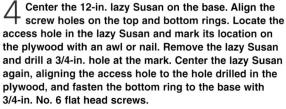

4 Center the 12-in. lazy Susan on the base. Align the screw holes on the top and bottom rings. Locate the access hole in the lazy Susan and mark its location on the plywood with an awl or nail. Remove the lazy Susan and drill a 3/4-in. hole at the mark. Center the lazy Susan again, aligning the access hole to the hole drilled in the plywood, and fasten the bottom ring to the base with 3/4-in. No. 6 flat head screws.

Handy Hints®

Mark the center line of each shelf on the opposite side of the dividers to help position the screws (Photo 3).

Anchor the base to the floor with masonry screws set in the exposed corners. Predrill the holes into the concrete with a 5/32-in. masonry bit or the size the screw package recommends.

The vinyl base provides an edge for the shelves. Buy the type that's not preglued. The 4-in.-wide type is most common, but buy the 3-in.-wide type if you can. Otherwise, use a sharp utility knife to trim an inch off the 4-in. one. Secure it to the edges of the curved plywood shelves using cove base adhesive and 1-in. tacks, as shown in Photo 9. Then load up your shelves and take them for a spin.

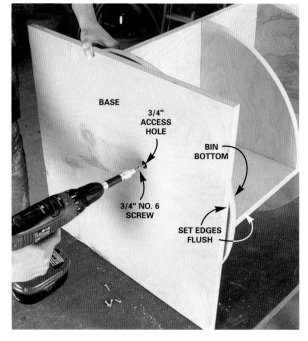

5 Center the base on the bin bottom and align a screw hole in the top ring of the lazy Susan with the access hole. Fasten the top ring of the lazy Susan to the bin bottom with a 3/4-in. No. 6 flat head screw driven through the access hole. Turn the bin bottom to align the remaining screw holes in the top ring with the access hole, and fasten with additional screws.

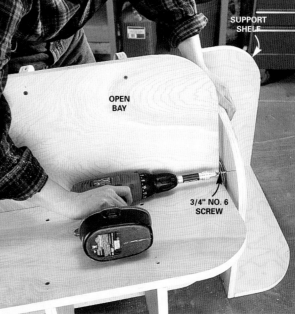

6 Screw the bottom ring of the 3-in. lazy Susan to the dividers on top of the bin with 3/4-in. screws. Assemble the support shelf (Figure A). Mark the bin rotation center on its bottom (about 13 in. from each wall) so the bin will clear the wall by about an inch when it rotates.

7 Center the 3-in. lazy Susan at the rotation center on the support shelf. Screw the top ring of the lazy Susan to the support shelf with the 3/4-in. screws.

8 Set the bin on treated 1x2s with the base about 1 in. from the walls. Shim to level if needed. Level the support shelf and screw it to the wall studs with 2-1/2-in. screws. Spin the bin to test for smooth operation. If it runs rough, shim the base or slide it side to side slightly until it spins smoothly. Predrill and fasten the base to the floor with 2-1/2-in. masonry screws.

9 Squeeze a 3/8-in. bead of cove base adhesive along the shelf edges. Position the vinyl base with the lip to the top, curling out. Secure the ends with 1-in. tacks. Trim the ends flush with a utility knife.

Plywood storage rack

A solution to the where-to-put-the-plywood problem

P lywood takes up relatively little space and is easy to store—simply lean it against a wall. The trick is getting at it when you need it. Nine times out of 10, you need the half sheet that's buried behind 12 others.

If you've experienced that frustration, you'll love this rack. Casters and a set of hinges are the secret for easy access. They allow you to swing the storage rack out from the wall and slide out the storm window, paneling or other item you want. Dividers strengthen the rack while enabling you to separate large sheets from smaller ones.

Each slot has room for about six sheets of 3/4-in. plywood. Although you can modify this design and make the slots larger, keep in mind that anything that sits around for a year or two is a donation candidate.

Construction of the rack goes surprisingly fast. Plan an afternoon for the project plus an hour or two to run to

project at a glance

skill level
beginner to intermediate

tools
circular saw
drill

cost
about $100

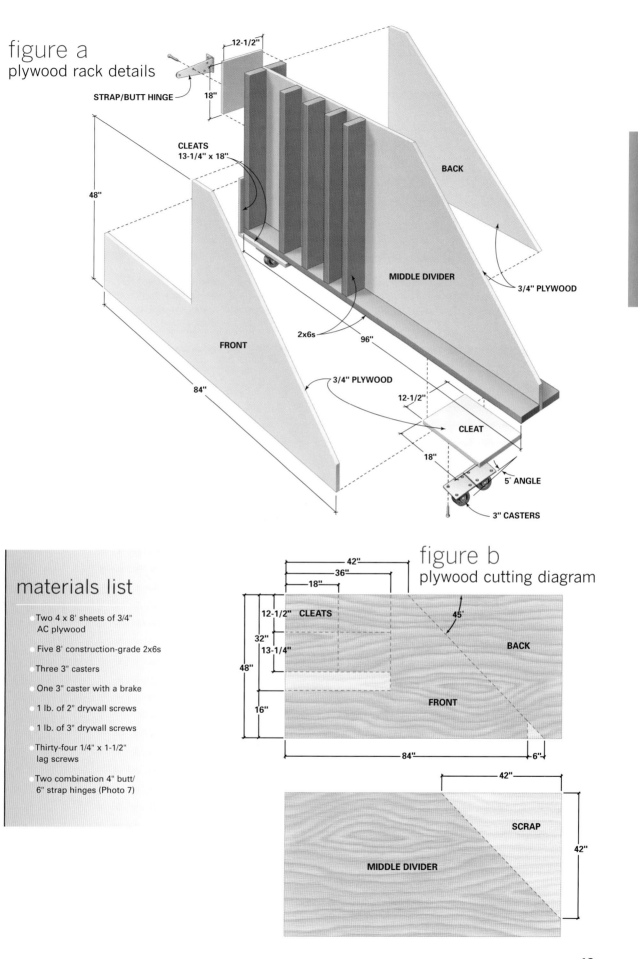

figure a
plywood rack details

12-1/2"

STRAP/BUTT HINGE

18"

CLEATS
13-1/4" x 18"

48"

BACK

3/4" PLYWOOD

MIDDLE DIVIDER

2x6s

96"

FRONT

3/4" PLYWOOD

84"

12-1/2"

CLEAT

18"

5° ANGLE

3" CASTERS

materials list

- Two 4 x 8' sheets of 3/4" AC plywood
- Five 8' construction-grade 2x6s
- Three 3" casters
- One 3" caster with a brake
- 1 lb. of 2" drywall screws
- 1 lb. of 3" drywall screws
- Thirty-four 1/4" x 1-1/2" lag screws
- Two combination 4" butt/ 6" strap hinges (Photo 7)

figure b
plywood cutting diagram

42"

36"

18"

12-1/2" CLEATS

45°

32"

13-1/4"

48"

BACK

16"

FRONT

84"

6"

42"

SCRAP

42"

MIDDLE DIVIDER

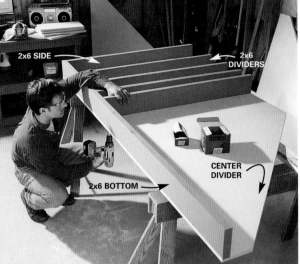

1 Cut plywood to the dimensions shown in Figure B. The cuts don't have to be precise; you don't need a saw guide. Wear goggles and hearing protection.

2 Cut the 2x6s to length and position them on the center plywood divider. Tack them to the plywood with 2-in. drywall screws driven from underneath. Then screw the 2x6 dividers to the bottom 2x6 with 3-in. drywall screws.

3 Lay the front plywood piece over the 2x6s and anchor it with 2-in. screws driven every 12 inches.

4 Flip the project over and assemble the back section. Position back 2x6s for the bottom and side and fasten them with two 3-in. screws where they meet. Then drive screws at an angle (toe-screw) through the ends of the 2x6s into the assembly below. Attach the plywood back piece to the 2x6s with the 2-in. screws.

the home center for materials. The least expensive wood will do, although for a few dollars more, an AC grade of plywood (sanded on one side) is usually flatter and nicer to work with.

When loaded, this rack is heavy, so make sure to buy casters rated for at least 200 lbs. each. One of the casters should have a brake for extra stability. If you purchase all your materials new, it'll cost a little over 100 bucks. But chances are you'll have some of these materials lying

around. (Use up that extra 3/4-in. plywood!)

Cut the plywood and 2x6s to size first, following Figure B, p. 13, for dimensions (Photo 1). You can make your cuts freehand (without a guideboard) because they don't have to be perfect. Use a sharp, carbide-tipped blade with at least 24 teeth to minimize splintering.

After cutting all the pieces, screw the rack together. Start with the center plywood divider first, attaching the bottom 2x6 and then the side. Use the factory edge of the

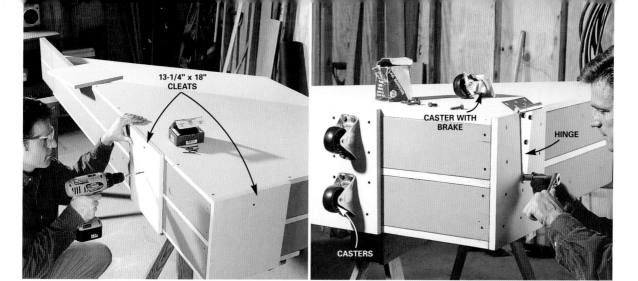

5 Fasten four plywood cleats to the bottom and sides with 2-in. screws to hold the rack together. Use 12 screws per cleat.

13-1/4" x 18" CLEATS

6 Attach the four casters and the strap leaf of the hinges with 1/4-in. x 1-1/2-in. lag screws. Place the caster with a brake on the outer front edge of the rack to hold the rack stationary when sliding items in and out.

CASTER WITH BRAKE
HINGE
CASTERS

7 Predrill pilot holes and fasten the rack to the wall stud with 1-1/2-in. lag screws.

WALL STUD
LAG SCREWS

8 Swing the rack out from the wall and load it with plywood, drywall and other big, flat stuff.

plywood to keep it all square. Next, measure and mark out your center 2x6 dividers and set them in place (Photo 2). This spacing isn't critical; use more or fewer dividers depending on your needs. After you fasten the front piece of plywood (Photo 3), you can turn the rack over and drive additional screws, spacing them every 12 inches. For the back bin you'll have to toe-screw (screw at an angle) the bottom and side 2x6s through the center plywood divider and into the opposite 2x6 (Photo 4). These

toe-screws hold them in place until you attach cleats, which solidly join the two sections (Photo 5).

All that's left is attaching the hardware and fastening the rack to the wall. Since the rack and its contents are heavy, use lag screws to hold the casters and hinges in place. Predrill your holes with a 3/16-in. bit. Set the casters at a slight angle (5 degrees) to accommodate the swing of the rack (Figure A, p. 13). Attach the hinges and you're all set to swing the rack out from the wall and fill it up.

Foldaway workshop

This space saver will keep your work area clutter free and your tools within reach

This workshop has loads of storage for all your gear and yet keeps it easily accessible. Best of all, when you're finished for the day, you can put everything away, shut the doors and lock it up. You'll also appreciate its modest profile. With the doors shut, it protrudes a mere 14-1/2 in. from the wall, so no sweat, you'll still be able to pull your car into the garage—and even get out.

This workshop is also designed to be easy to build with simple woodworking tools. In fact, all you'll need besides your measuring and marking tools is a circular saw, a jigsaw and a drill. And it doesn't have any tricky wood joints to slow down the building process—just screws and nails. If you have basic carpentry skills, you'll find you can easily work your way through the how-to steps in a single weekend. You'll also like the price; the whole thing will only cost you about $300.

You'll be able to buy everything at a home center except the folding L-brackets. These heavy-duty brackets will support up to 750 lbs. and you'll find they live up to the claim. The brackets have four positions: straight up for tabletop work and flat down for storage, as well as two

in-between locking positions that transform the worktop into a handy drawing board. Check Resources on p. 250 for a mail-order source.

Besides the fold-down worktop, you'll appreciate the adjustable shelves in each door recess that'll hold boxes of nails and screws, paint, glue bottles, spare parts—you name it. And the sturdy piano hinges are strong enough to hold nearly anything you can pack into the shelves. The tried-and-true peg board is great for visually organizing your hand tools, and space for an overhead fluorescent light and an outlet strip for power tools is included. There's plenty of room on the bottom shelf for bigger tools like your circular saw, belt sander and router. The foldaway workshop is also great for hobby, craft and even gardening supplies and tools. So whether you're building one or several, get your materials and follow the step-by-step photos and clear shop drawing.

Choose straight lumber

Go to a home center and choose your lumber carefully. The main frame of the project is built with sturdy, dry, construction-grade 2x10s and 2x4s. Buy them as straight as you can find. If they have a twist or bow, they'll throw off the frame and the doors will be difficult to fit. The plywood should be 3/4 in. and flat. You can get by with construction grade, but we used birch plywood because it's nice looking and perfectly flat. The door sides and shelves should be hardwood for strength. Many home centers have a nice selection of maple to match the birch plywood. You can substi-

shopping list

DESCRIPTION	QTY.
2x10 x 8' spruce, pine or fir	3
2x4 x 14' spruce, pine or fir	1
2x2 x 8' spruce, pine or fir	1
1x6 x 12' hardwood (door sides and shelves)	4
1x8 x 4' pine shelf (under-bracket blocks)	1
37" x 44-15/16" peg board (1/4" thick)	1
3/4" x 4' x 8' birch plywood	2
1x2 x 12' hardwood worktop edging	1
6' piano hinges	2
6' shelf standards and brackets	8
1/4" x 1-3/4" x 10' pine or hardwood lattice (shelf edging)	2
6d nails	1 lb.
3" wood screws	2 lbs.
2-1/2" wood screws	1 lb.
1-5/8" wood screws	1 lb.
1-1/4" wood screws	1 lb.
1/4" x 4" lag screws and washers	6
Folding L-brackets (see Resources, p. 186)	1 pr.
Magnetic catches (see Resources, p. 186)	2
Wall anchors, bolt snaps, door handles	
Mini-tube fluorescent light	1

cutting list

KEY	PCS.	SIZE & DESCRIPTION
A	2	1-1/2" x 9" x 78" pine sides
B	3	1-1/2" x 3-1/2" x 48" pine stretchers
C	2	1-1/2" x 9" x 45" pine top and bottom
D1	2	1-1/2" x 1-1/2" x 33-1/2" pine backers for peg-board
D2	1	1/4" x 44-15/16" x 37" peg board
E1	2	1-1/2" x 6-1/8" x 12-3/4" pine bracket supports
E2	1	3/4" x 6-1/8" x 45" fixed pine shelf
F	4	3/4" x 5-1/2" x 73" maple door sides
G	4	3/4" x 5-1/2" x 23-7/8" maple door tops and bottoms
H	2	3/4" x 22-3/8" x 73" birch plywood door panels
J	2	3/4" x 22-3/8" x 43-3/8" birch plywood worktop pieces
K1	2	3/4" x 1-1/2" x 22-3/8" maple
K2	2	3/4" x 1-1/2" x 44-7/8" maple
L1	10	3/4" x 4-7/16" x 22-3/8" maple shelves
L2	10	1/4" x 1-3/4" x 22-1/4" maple shelf stops
M	2	3/4" x 5-1/2" maple triangular braces

figure a
workbench assembly

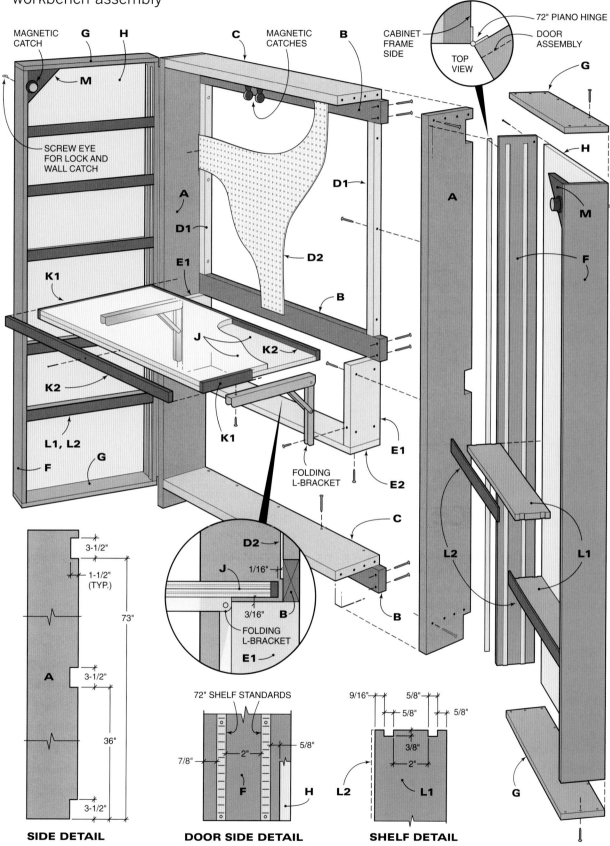

MAGNETIC CATCH **G** **H**

M

SCREW EYE FOR LOCK AND WALL CATCH

C MAGNETIC CATCHES **B**

72" PIANO HINGE

CABINET FRAME SIDE

TOP VIEW

DOOR ASSEMBLY

G

H

A

D1

D1

D2

A

M

B

F

K1

E1

J

K2

B

K2

K1

L1, L2

F **G**

FOLDING L-BRACKET

E1

E2

L2

L1

C

D2

J 1/16"

3/16" **B**

FOLDING L-BRACKET

E1

B

B

G

SIDE DETAIL

3-1/2"

1-1/2" (TYP.)

73"

A

3-1/2"

36"

3-1/2"

DOOR SIDE DETAIL

72" SHELF STANDARDS

7/8"

2"

5/8"

F

H

SHELF DETAIL

9/16" 5/8"

5/8" 5/8"

3/8"

2"

L2

L1

1 Rip 2x10 lumber to 9 in. wide to create a flat edge and ensure that all the frame pieces are uniform. Then mark and cut the 1-1/2-in.-deep notches for the rear stretcher pieces (Figure A).

2 Set the rear stretchers (B) into the notches of the sides (A) and screw them into place. Next, screw the top and bottom pieces (C) to the sides and stretchers.

making it fit your space

There may be a few snags to look out for in your garage. If you're installing the foldaway workshop near the garage door, make sure it will clear the track. The height of the project is 78 inches. Low-clearance overhead doors may have a track in the way. Also keep in mind that it opens to a full 8 feet. You'll find you still have 3-1/2 in. behind the doors when they're open so you can hang rakes and shovels behind it.

Your garage may have a row of concrete block near the floor that sticks out past the wall surface. If so, plan ahead and cut the side pieces longer past the bottom stretcher to accommodate the block and then notch them to fit around it. Also feel free to make the project shorter or a bit taller to suit your needs and adjust the worktop to a height that suits you. The one shown sits at a comfortable 36 in. off the floor.

tute poplar, oak or birch. Here again, make sure the lumber is straight. Boards that aren't perfectly straight can be cut up for the shorter shelves.

NOTE: Assemble the project on an even, flat surface. You can end up with some unintentional twists in the main frame and the doors if you build them on an uneven surface. Choose a flat area in your garage or driveway for the assembly work.

Notches in the frame keep it square

Ripping your 2x10s to 9 in. wide gives you a nice, square edge on the face of the frame to mount your piano hinges to later. Once they're ripped, notch the back of the frame sides as shown in Photo 1 to accept the horizontal stretchers. Set your saw to a 1-1/2-in. depth of cut and make multiple passes, about 1/4 in. apart, across the width of the 2x4. Break out the notches with a chisel and file the bottom of the notches smooth.

Take care to get the frame square as you screw the

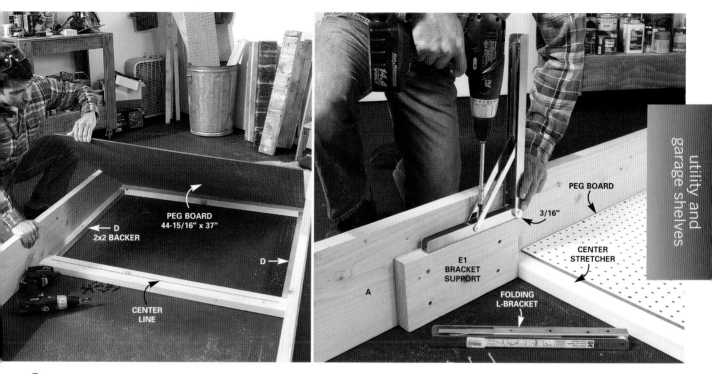

3 Flip the assembly over onto its back. Measure and cut a pair of 2x2 backers to fit between the center and upper stretchers. Next, screw the peg board to stretchers and the 2x2s.

4 Screw the folding L-bracket supports (E1) to the sides. Position the brackets 3/16 in. past the top of the support and flush with the support's inside edge. Screw the brackets into the support with No. 8 x 1-1/4-in. pan head screws.

stretchers (B) into the notches and screw the top and bottom panels (C) into place. The best way to ensure the frame is square is to measure the diagonals and adjust the frame until they're equal.

The peg board stiffens the frame

Once you've got the basic frame assembled, cut your peg board and center it onto the top and middle stretchers. You'll know in a hurry if your frame is out of square because the panel should fall into place (Photo 3). Fasten the peg board every 6 in. to the stretchers and 2x2s with 1-1/4-in. wood screws.

L-brackets make a rock-solid top

Position the brackets carefully as you install them on the bracket supports to make sure they'll open and close once the project is complete. Keep them flush with the inside edge of the supports and make sure they extend 3/16 in. past the top (Photo 4). This little extension gives a

bit of room for the folding L-brackets to release properly when it's time to fold them down.

Take the same care later (Photo 9) when you attach the top to the folding L-brackets. Make sure the top is 1/16 in. from the peg board and that the tops of the L-brackets are parallel to the sides of the worktop.

Install the shelf standards precisely

The shelf standards support the shelves, and the notches in the shelves hold them in place so they don't fly out when you open the door. Set your combination square to the dimensions shown in Figure A, p. 19, and slide it up along the edge of the door frame sides (F) as you nail the standards into place. Also make sure you flush the standard bottoms to the bottom of the door sides so all the shelves will be level.

Rip your shelves to width and again be precise with the layout of the notches in the ends of the shelf. These are a bugger to cut, but making multiple passes from each

5 Cut the door frame sides (F) and top and bottom pieces (G) to length from 1x6 boards. Position the 6-ft. shelf standards flush with the bottom edge of each door side (F) and nail them every 6 inches.

6 Cut the door panels (H) and place them into a cradle brace as shown. Spread glue on the edge of the plywood and predrill and nail the sides (F) to the plywood door panels every 6 inches. Once the sides are fastened, predrill and glue and screw the door tops and bottoms (G) to the door panels.

end with a jigsaw works well. You can clean up the cuts with a file.

Cutting your plywood door panels

Use a table saw to first rip the panels for a nice, straight edge. If you don't have a table saw, use a circular saw and a long straightedge guide. Once the panels are cut for width, mark the length using a framing square as a guide. Cut each panel carefully with your circular saw equipped with a sharp 40-tooth blade.

Attach the door sides, making sure they're flush with the plywood door panel face. If a little glue oozes out, wipe it off with a wet rag right away to keep it from showing through your finish later.

Screw the top and bottom of the door frame (parts G) to the panel (H) instead of nailing them. The 1-5/8-in. screws, along with the glue, bond the door sides and plywood panel together for a rock-solid door. To complete the door frame, cut a pair of triangular pieces of maple (M) 5-1/2 in. on a side and glue and nail them to the top inside corners of the doors to hold the closing plates of the magnetic door catches.

Piano hinges give total door support

Piano hinges can be a pain to install, but you can simplify the process by tucking the top flap between the door and the frame (Photo 7) to hold it in place while you screw the lower exposed flap to the frame side. To predrill perfectly centered holes, use a No. 3 Vix bit in your drill. This nifty bit has a tapered front edge that fits into the hole on the hinge and exactly centers itself. As you push on the bit, the spring-loaded bit pilots itself dead center. Drive the screws as you go to keep the hinge from shifting.

Once the bottom flap of the hinge is secured, lift the door, pivot the top flat out, position the door side even with the frame and secure the hinge to the door frame.

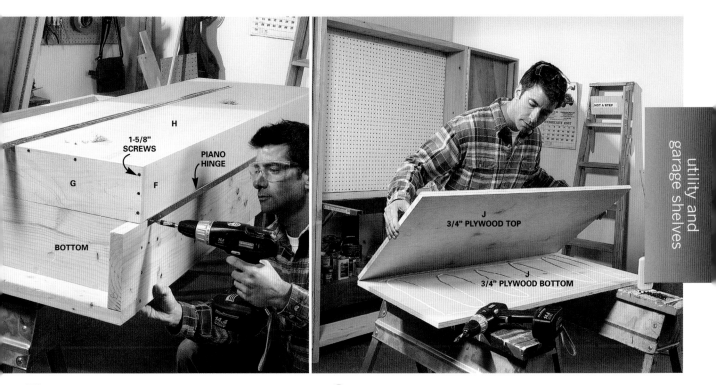

H

1-5/8" SCREWS

PIANO HINGE

G **F**

BOTTOM

J 3/4" PLYWOOD TOP

J 3/4" PLYWOOD BOTTOM

7 Set the door assemblies onto the frame assembly as shown. Fold the top flap of your piano hinge so it's trapped between the door edge and the side of the frame to position it evenly. Screw it to the frame, then open the hinge and screw it to the door.

8 Cut and glue two pieces of 3/4-in. plywood (J) to make the work surface. To complete the worktop, cut 1x2 boards to length and nail them to the sides with 6d finish nails.

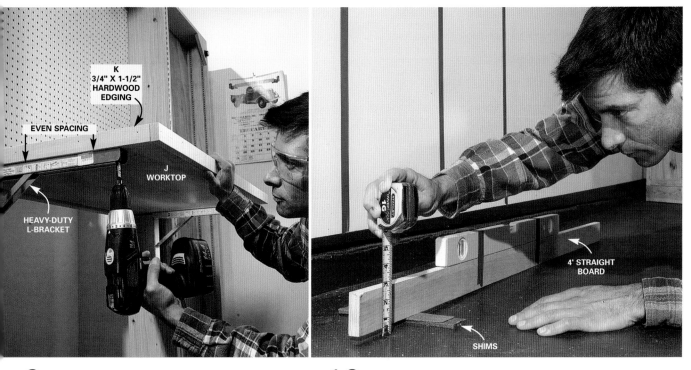

K 3/4" X 1-1/2" HARDWOOD EDGING

EVEN SPACING

J WORKTOP

HEAVY-DUTY L-BRACKET

4' STRAIGHT BOARD

SHIMS

9 Center the worktop (J) between the sides and leave a 1/16-in. gap from the face of the peg board. Make sure the folding L-brackets are evenly spaced front-to-back along the edge of the worktop. Screw the L-bracket to the underside of the worktop with No. 8 x 1-1/4-in. pan head screws.

10 Check your floor with a level placed on a 4-ft. board to see how much you may need to shim the cabinet sides. This garage floor had a 1/2-in. slope in 4 ft., from front to back.

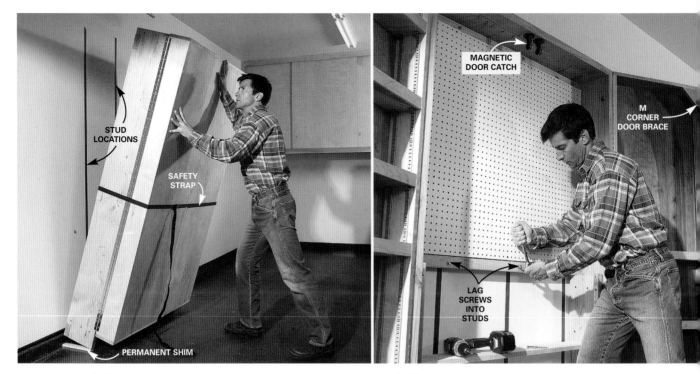

STUD LOCATIONS

SAFETY STRAP

PERMANENT SHIM

MAGNETIC DOOR CATCH

M CORNER DOOR BRACE

LAG SCREWS INTO STUDS

11 Mark the stud locations. Cut and set the shim. Tip the cabinet up slowly with the doors closed. Slide it into position.

12 Drill 3/16-in. pilot holes through the stretchers into the studs. Insert 1/4-in. x 4-in. lag screws and washers and use a wrench to tighten the cabinet to the wall. Add the magnetic catches and the shelves.

Use a double layer of plywood for a solid worktop

Cut your worktop pieces (J) from 3/4-in. plywood and glue them (Photo 8) together with carpenter's glue spread liberally between. Screw the pieces together on the underside with 1-1/4-in. wood screws. Once the glue sets, cut 1x2 maple and nail it around the edges (Figure A, p. 19).

Position the top carefully onto the folding L-brackets. Hold the top securely, align the brackets parallel to the edge and screw it into place. You'll need a bit extension for your power screwdriver to get inside the bracket mechanism. If you don't have one, you can mark it, predrill it and then use a long-blade screwdriver to drive the screws. At this point, test the mechanism to make sure it folds down. If the bracket binds, loosen the screws and shift the bracket until it works.

Lag-screw the frame to the studs

Every installation situation has its own set of problems, and the one shown here was no exception. The floor was out of level, so one side had to be shimmed to get the project to sit level on the floor. The concrete foundation at the bottom of the wall stuck out 1/2 in., so 1/2-in. strips were added to the backside of the frame to move it out from the wall a bit. Use your ingenuity to get past any problems you might find. Here some bolt snaps were secured to the wall (see top small photo, p. 25) with wall anchors and screw eyes to keep the doors open when in use. The screw eyes on the front of the door also double as a place to slip in a padlock to keep out unwanted visitors.

Caution: The doors of this project can fly open when you're moving it into position. Use a strap hinge and brace the bottom of the doors until you get it secured to the wall.

Flip the top down, close the doors and secure the padlock until you're ready for your next project.

Finishing touches

The magnetic catches for the doors are actually interior door catches (see Resources, p. 186). Screw the ball section to the top of the frame and the steel plate onto the door. Locate a mini-tube fluorescent light fixture at a home center and screw it to the underside of the top. An outlet strip mounted to the side of the frame makes plugging in power tools a snap. Drill a 1-1/2-in. hole in the frame side to slip the plug end through to the nearest outlet.

Although not completely necessary, two coats of furniture oil or polyurethane will help preserve the project, especially if your garage gets seasonally damp. Just remove the hardware and apply your finish. Be sure to wait a couple of days for the project to dry before using it.

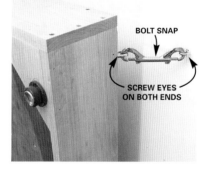

Keep the doors open with a wall anchor and double-ended bolt snap.

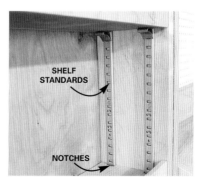

The notches in the shelves keep them secure as you open and close your doors.

Multipurpose towers
Keep everything organized with versatile shelves, bins and drawers

This versatile storage system is the ultimate all-purpose odds and ends organizer for your garage. It's composed of tall, shallow towers that hold a wide variety of adjustable shelves and bins. By installing the towers along the same wall, you can add a range of special storage features between them—notched shelves for skis and fishing rods, pairs of dowels to corral balls, brackets for the trolling motor, and more (photo below). The tower shelves can be crafted into bins, tote boxes or almost any other accessory you can imagine (Photos 8 – 10). Here' you'll learn how to build the basic tower framework and a few custom accessories. You can devise variations to fit your storage needs.

The materials for the three towers cost just short of $200. The towers and shelves go together relatively quickly—you can easily build three in a day. Allow an

additional day for 10 or so bins, depending on how detailed you choose to make them. They're well worth the extra effort.

The cabinets are constructed of 3/4-in. birch plywood. The cleats and back are made of 1/2-in. MDF (medium-density fiberboard).

Assembly details

Start by cutting the plywood for the cabinet, following the dimensions shown in Figure A, p. 29. Use a circular saw and a straightedge for accuracy (Photo 1). Then cut the tops and bottoms of the cabinet 1/2 in. narrower than the sides (Figure A). Because of the cutting waste, you can only cut four 11-7/8-in.-wide pieces from a 4-ft.-wide sheet of plywood. One 4 x 8-ft. sheet will make two tower frames with sawdust left over.

Next cut a sheet of 1/2-in. MDF (Figure A) to make the back, cleats and shelves. After cutting the cleats and back, you'll have enough stock remaining for four shelves from each sheet. Cut your shelves to length after you've assembled the cabinet. Then double-check your measurements and cut the shelves to fit a little loose so they'll slide easily.

Make the jig shown in Photo 2 to cut the cleats fast and accurately. Screw a 24-in. 2x4 perfectly perpendicular to the edge of a scrap of plywood. (Check it with a framing square.) Then screw a 1/4-in. stop block to the 2x4 so the cut-off distance is 5-3/8 inches.

Caution: Don't use a stop block thicker than 1/4 in. or the cleat might pinch the saw blade, making the saw kick back.

Cut 12 cleats from each 11-3/8-in. x 8-ft. length of MDF, leaving about 30 in. for a shelf. Screw the cleats to the plywood sides (Photo 3), positioning your first cleat

1 Cut the plywood sides, tops and bottoms according to the dimensions in Figure A. Clamp a straightedge to the plywood as a saw guide to ensure straight, accurate cuts.

2 Rip two 11-3/8-in. x 8-ft. pieces from the MDF and cut cleats plus one shelf from each. Assemble a simple jig from a 2x4 and an MDF shelf (or plywood scrap) to ensure square cuts and speed up the job. Cut the back and shelves from the remaining piece of MDF.

making it fit your space

MDF definitely has its pros and cons. First the pros. It's more stable than plywood, so it stays flat. It cuts and machines incredibly easily with little chipping or splintering. Because it's also kind of slippery, it works great for the smooth sliding bins and shelves in this project. And it's cheaper than plywood. But MDF has a couple of drawbacks. It doesn't tolerate moisture. If the cabinets get rain soaked or you live in an extremely humid area, you should seal the MDF (and entire cabinet) with polyurethane.

MDF works great, but if you're a die-hard plywood fan, go ahead and use that instead.

3/4 in. up from the bottom edge to allow space for the plywood bottom. Recess the drywall screwheads in the MDF so the bins won't get hung up on them. MDF is so hard that the screws will snap if you try to drive them flush. Create the recess with a counterbore bit (Photo 3 inset), which you can buy at any hardware store for about $2. Position the top cleat down 3/4 in. from the top of each side panel to leave room for the plywood top.

To simplify attaching the cleats to the second side, clamp both sides back to back and flush top and bottom (Photo 3). Use a spacer long enough to bridge both sides. This ensures that all your shelves and bins will line up.

TIP: Before you remove the clamps, label both sides so you don't confuse them with another pair.

The tedious part is over. Now assemble the cabinet sides, top, bottom and back (Photo 4), working on a flat floor where you have plenty of space. In addition, drive a couple of screws through the back into the cleats near the middle to keep the sides from bowing. Predrill the screw holes with a 1/8-in. bit so you don't split the narrow 1/2-in. cleats.

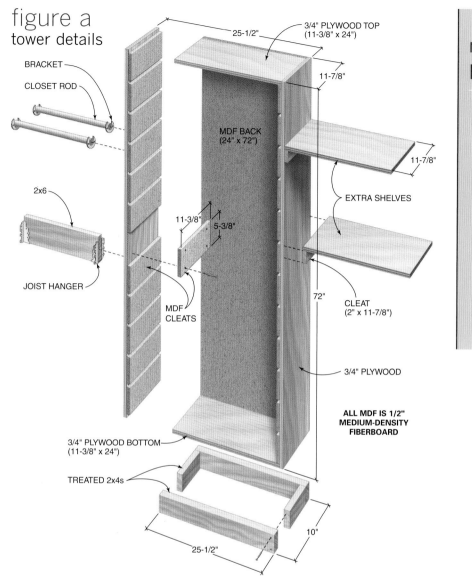

figure a
tower details

BRACKET

CLOSET ROD

2x6

JOIST HANGER

25-1/2"

3/4" PLYWOOD TOP
(11-3/8" x 24")

11-7/8"

MDF BACK
(24" x 72")

11-7/8"

EXTRA SHELVES

11-3/8"

5-3/8"

MDF
CLEATS

72"

CLEAT
(2" x 11-7/8")

3/4" PLYWOOD

3/4" PLYWOOD BOTTOM
(11-3/8" x 24")

TREATED 2x4s

25-1/2"

10"

**ALL MDF IS 1/2"
MEDIUM-DENSITY
FIBERBOARD**

materials list

You'll need the following materials to build three towers:

- Two 4 x 8' sheets of 3/4" birch plywood
- Three 4 x 8' sheets of 1/2" MDF (medium-density fiberboard)
- One 4 x 8' sheet of 1/2" MDF for bins
- Three 6' pressure-treated 2x4s
- 1 lb. of 1" drywall screws
- 1 lb. of 2" drywall screws
- 1 lb. of 3" drywall screws

Install the towers

If you rest the plywood tower directly on a concrete floor, it'll absorb moisture and the plywood will swell. Instead, set the cabinet on a pressure-treated 2x4 frame (Photo 5). Make the frame the same width as the tower (25-1/2 in.) but narrower in depth (about 10 in.) to provide a recessed toe-kick, as in a kitchen cabinet. Either nail or screw the frame pieces together with 3-in. fasteners.

Finally, mount the tower on the frame (Photo 5) and check it for plumb. Important: Screw the tower through the back into the wall studs so it doesn't tip over.

Customize for special uses

The space between towers is just as useful as the room inside them. Install a pair of closet poles 6 to 8 in. apart between two cabinets to hold soccer balls, basketballs or footballs (Photo 6). Hang a 2x8 on edge with a couple of joist hangers to hold a boat or trolling motor. Or simply cut 3/4-in. plywood shelves to various sizes and shapes for other special items.

Then build bins for the smaller stuff (Photo 7). Photos 8 – 10 and Figures B, C and D, p. 31, show handy, easy-to-build bin styles. Cut in a few handholds and you can carry the stuff right to where you're working (Photo 8). Insert a dowel through the side of a bin and you have a tote you

3 Screw the cleats to the plywood sides with four 1-in. drywall screws. Hold the cleat flush to the front edge of the cabinet. Use a scrap piece of shelf material plus a cereal box top as spacers. Use a counterbore bit to provide a recess for the drywall screws (inset photo).

4 Assemble the towers by driving three 2-in. drywall screws through the sides and into each edge of the top and bottom. Then screw on the back to square up and stiffen the cabinet (Figure A).

5 Cut and nail together a 2x4 frame for each tower. Position the frames, level them using shims and screw them to the wall with 3-in. screws. Then tip each tower onto a frame. Fasten each tower to wall studs with at least four 2-in. drywall screws.

6 Space additional towers at least 2 ft. apart. Then screw cleats, closet rod hangers and other types of supports to the outside faces of the sides to support more shelves and other storage devices.

7 Slide in the shelves. Build and insert the bins between the cleats according to our photos and plans (Figures B, C and D).

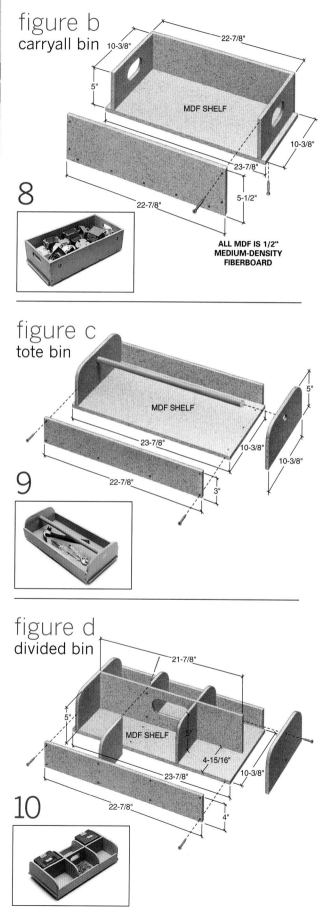

figure b
carryall bin

10-3/8" 22-7/8"

5"

MDF SHELF

10-3/8"

23-7/8"

5-1/2"

22-7/8"

8

ALL MDF IS 1/2"
MEDIUM-DENSITY
FIBERBOARD

figure c
tote bin

5"

MDF SHELF

23-7/8" 10-3/8"

10-3/8"

9

22-7/8"

3"

figure d
divided bin

21-7/8"

5"

MDF SHELF 5"

4-15/16"

23-7/8" 10-3/8"

10

22-7/8"

4"

can carry with one hand (Photo 9). Set dividers through the bin and for the first time in 35 years you'll have nails and screws that actually have a place they can call home (Photo 10). Combine this with a cutout for a handle and you've made them a mobile home.

The secret to assembling bins is to begin with a shelf with 1 in. cut off the long side. This shelf is the bottom. Then cut the ends, fronts and backs and screw and glue them to the bottom (Photos 8 – 10 and Figures B, C and D). Place dividers and handholds wherever they work best. Be sure to predrill all your screw holes, staying at least an inch away from the ends so you won't split the 1/2-in. MDF pieces.

If you have a router table and finish nailer as well as some spare time, you can really go design crazy. Setting the dividers into routed grooves adds strength. Use your imagination and you'll come up with all kinds of other ideas for customizing this system.

Under-sink shelf

Tired of moving all that stuff under the sink every time you mop the floor? Just buy a Melamine closet shelf from a home center and a length of suspended-ceiling wall angle (sorry, it only comes in 10-ft. lengths, but it's cheap and you can have it cut for transport). Also pick up four 1/2-in. No. 8-24 bolts, washers and nuts.

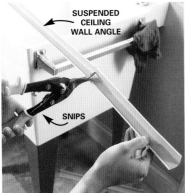

1 Using snips, cut two lengths of suspended ceiling wall angle to support the undersink shelf.

2 Clamp pieces of ceiling angle or aluminum angle to your sink legs (about 11 in. from the floor) and drill through with a 3/16-in. bit. Insert 1/2-in.-long No. 8-24 bolts from the inside and thread on acorn nuts to cover sharp bolt edges.

3 Cut a shelf from 3/4-in. Melamine board and drop it onto the angle braces. You may need to notch your shelf if the sink trap is in your way. Paint the raw edges of the board to protect them from moisture.

Upside-down shelves

Here's some neat and fast storage for your shop's upper regions. Bolt together a set of inexpensive metal shelves (about $12 at a home center) and attach them upside down to the ceiling joists with lag bolts. The spacing between shelves is completely adjustable. Hang the shelves so they're easy to reach, or set them high so you won't bonk your head. Trim the shelf posts to just the right height with tin snips.

TRIM POSTS TO LENGTH AND ATTACH TO JOISTS

ADJUSTABLE HEIGHT SHELVES

BUILT-IN LIP PREVENTS ITEMS FROM FALLING OFF SHELF!

Behind-the-stairs storage

That awkward space under the basement steps can easily be turned into a set of deep shelves perfect for storing everything from tools to shop vacuums, and of course, lumber. Help your small shop seem a lot bigger by using this highly underutilized space.

NOTCH PLYWOOD SHELF AROUND CENTER STRINGER

Ceiling drawers

To eke out every cubic inch of storage in a basement shop, try these boxes that hang between your ceiling joists. When a drawer is down, you have easy access to

its contents. A lag screw or bolt works well for a pivot and a pair of pivoting cleats holds each drawer in place. They're perfect for tools and supplies you don't need to access often.

Utility shelves

This sturdy, freestanding shelf unit is made from any inexpensive 1-by lumber (3/4 in. thick) for the legs, and plywood or particleboard for the shelves. Glue and nail the four L-shaped legs together with 6d finish nails. Clamp the shelves in place, getting them evenly spaced and level, then secure each shelf with eight 2-in. screws through the legs.

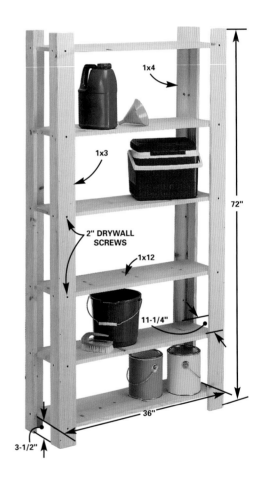

Mobile stacking totes

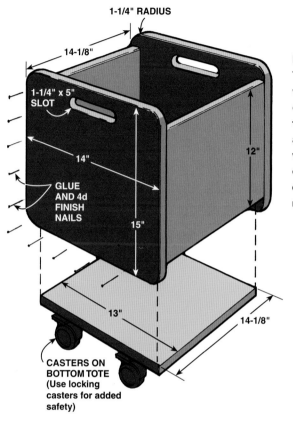

1-1/4" RADIUS

14-1/8"

1-1/4" x 5" SLOT

14"

12"

GLUE AND 4d FINISH NAILS

15"

13"

14-1/8"

CASTERS ON BOTTOM TOTE
(Use locking casters for added safety)

Make these stacking totes from 1/2-in. birch veneer plywood. The dimensions given here allow each tote to interlock snugly with the one above and below it. You can cut four totes from one full sheet of plywood—five from about a sheet and a third. Cut all the plywood parts to size, cut out the hand grips and sand all edges smooth. Then glue and assemble the totes with 4d finish nails. Leave them unfinished or apply paint or stain. Mount 2-in. casters on the bottom tote to make the stack mobile.

Up-and-away storage

The perfect place to store small quantities of long, narrow offcuts and moldings is right over your head. Build this set of overhead storage racks either in high basement ceilings or in the open trusses in garage shops. Use 2x6s for the vertical hangers and doubled-up 3/4-in. plywood for the lower angled supports. Secure each 2x6 into the framing with two 5/16-in. x 3-in. lag screws. Screw each hanger into the 2x6 with two offset 5/16-in. x 3-in. lags. The angle on the supports keeps stuff from sliding off.

2x6 HANGER

PLYWOOD SUPPORT

kitchen and bathroom storage

Roll-out pantry 38

Corner swing- and
    roll-out trays 41

Space-saving cabinet 44

Door-mounted spice and
    lid racks 48

Pull-out trash drawer 50

Toe-kick drawers 52

Roll-out kitchen trays 54

Afternoon projects

    Open kitchen shelves 58

    Glass shelves 59

Gallery of ideas 60

Roll-out pantry

Twice the storage with half the hassle

M ost cabinet manufacturers now include roll-out shelves in their base cabinets. But if you don't have this convenience, this project will one-up those shelves. Here's how to make an entire roll-out pantry.

The hardware consists of two heavy-duty bottom-mounted slides (see Resources, p. 186) and one center-mounted top slide that together can support 130 lbs. Construct your unit to suit your needs. This bottom tray is 3-1/2 in. tall and the upper ones are 2-1/2 in. tall. You may want to include only two trays if you'll be storing cereal boxes and other tall packages.

Since you'll be converting your door from swinging to rolling mode, you'll need to remove the door and hinges. You'll also have to remove the existing handle, fill the screw holes with putty and rein-stall the pull centered on the door. If your hardware mounts from the backside, install it before attaching the door (Photo 6).

project at a glance

skill level
intermediate

tools
circular saw
miter saw
drill

cost
about $30 for wood; about $60 for roll-out pantry hardware

1 Measure the cabinet face frame opening, then subtract the height of the top and bottom glides. Use the guidelines given to arrive at the depth, width and height of your pantry unit. Be sure to install the bottom glides so they run parallel to the cabinet sides. If necessary, use plywood to raise the cabinet bottom even with the bottom lip of the face frame.

2 Install the top glide support and top glide so the support is level and flush to the top of the frame opening. Screw plywood flanges to each end of the 1x3 support beforehand to make it simpler to secure it to the front and back of the cabinet.

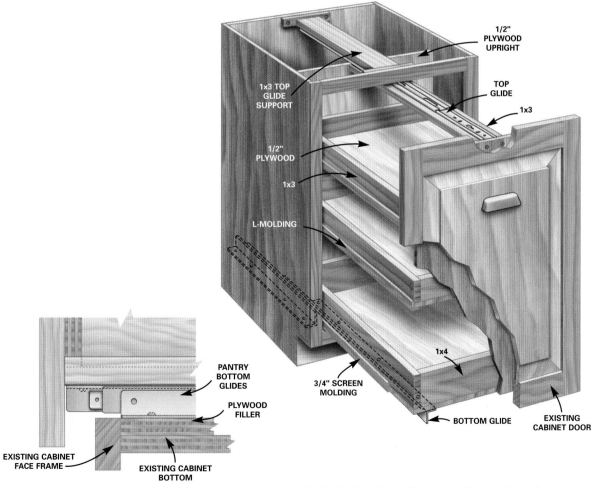

● Shelf unit dimensions will vary according to cabinet size.

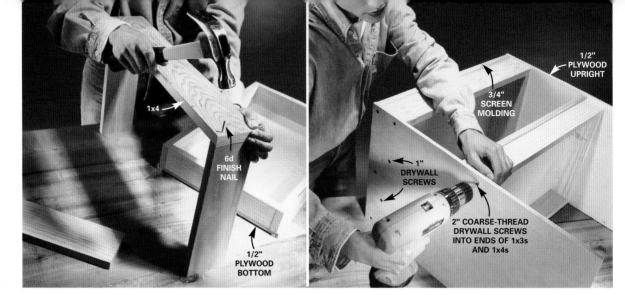

3 Assemble the pantry trays using 1x4s, 1x3s, 6d nails and carpenter's glue. Use the plywood bottoms to square up the trays before nailing them on. L-moldings support and cover the plywood edges of the upper two trays; 3/4-in. screen molding covers the exposed plywood edges of the bottom tray.

4 Secure the trays to the 1/2-in. plywood uprights using glue and drywall screws. Arrange the spacing of the trays to meet your needs.

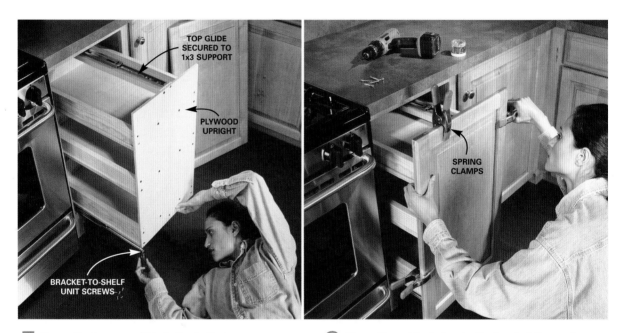

5 Screw the tray assembly to the bottom runners, making sure it's centered in the opening and running parallel to the cabinet sides. The extended portion of the top slide is secured to a 1x3 screwed between the two plywood uprights. You can loosen this 1x3, then adjust the height so the top glide runs flat and smooth.

6 Clamp the cabinet door to the front of the pantry assembly; center it and make the height even with adjacent doors. Predrill eight holes through the plywood upright and drive screws into the back of the cabinet door. After installing two screws, close the door to check its alignment with the adjacent doors. Make adjustments, then install the remaining screws. Use short screws so they don't penetrate the front of the cabinet door.

The key measurements and clearances for the roll-out unit are as follows: The plywood front and back panels should be about 1/8 in. shorter than the distance between the installed top and bottom glides (see illustration on p. 39). The width of the unit should be 1/2 in. narrower than the cabinet opening. The depth of the unit should be 1/2 in. less than the depth of the cabinet (not including the face frame).

Corner swing- and roll-out trays

Better access for hard-to-reach corners

Blind-corner cabinets—those with a blank face that allow another cabinet to butt into them—may be great for aging wine, but they're darn near impossible to see and reach into. This pair of accessories puts an end to this hidden wasteland. The hinged shelf swings out of the way, and the gliding shelf slides forward so you can access food items stored in the back. You

project at a glance

skill level
intermediate

tools
miter saw
drill

cost
about $40

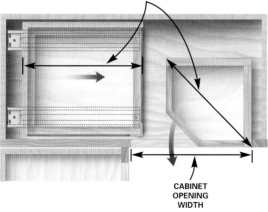

● These two measurements cannot exceed cabinet opening width.

CABINET OPENING WIDTH

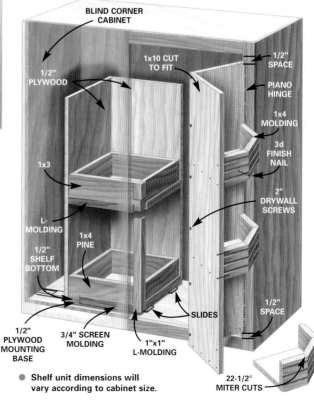

BLIND CORNER CABINET

1/2" PLYWOOD

1x10 CUT TO FIT

1/2" SPACE

PIANO HINGE

1x4 MOLDING

3d FINISH NAIL

2" DRYWALL SCREWS

1x3

L-MOLDING

1/2" SHELF BOTTOM

1x4 PINE

1/2" SPACE

SLIDES

1/2" PLYWOOD MOUNTING BASE

3/4" SCREEN MOLDING

1"x1" L-MOLDING

22-1/2° MITER CUTS

● Shelf unit dimensions will vary according to cabinet size.

1 Glue and nail the 1x3s together using 4d finish nails, then use 3d finish nails to secure the plywood bottom.

2 Cut out the two plywood sides, then glue and nail the corners. Connect the trays to the two plywood sides using 1-in. drywall screws, then cut and nail L-molding to support the front corner. Cut and install L-moldings to support and cover the exposed plywood edges of the upper tray. Install 3/4-in. screen molding to cover the plywood edges of the bottom tray.

can use the same hardware and techniques for making base cabinets more accessible, too.

The key measurements and clearances:

Glide-out shelf dimensions. You can make the unit only as long as the door opening is wide (or else you can't fit it in). Make the unit about 1/2 in. narrower than the inside width of the cabinet.

Swing-out tray dimensions. The corner-to-corner or diagonal measurement of the unit (see p. 41) can't exceed the width of the door opening (or else that won't fit either). Make the unit about 1 in. shorter than the opening height so it has room to swing freely when installed.

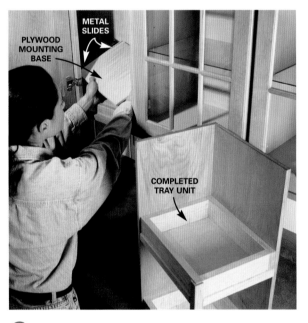

3 Cut the mounting base plywood slightly smaller than the other tray bottoms, then secure the two slides parallel to each other about 1 in. from each edge. Slip this mounting base into the opening, extend the slides, then screw them to the cabinet bottom at the rear of the cabinet. Install the slides parallel to the cabinet sides, so the base slides back and forth freely.

Handy Hints

● Beg, borrow or rent a compressor, finish nailer and brad gun, if you can. You'll work faster, eliminate hammer marks and split the wood less often than you would hand-nailing.

● Use a damp sponge to wipe up glue drips immediately. It'll save hours of sanding down the line.

● Test-fit your shelf units in the cabinet as you work.

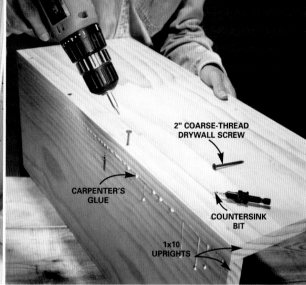

4 Screw the tray unit to the mounting base using 3/4-in. screws. After installing the first screw, slide the unit forward and back, then adjust it until it runs parallel to the cabinet sides and install three more screws.

5 Cut the 1x10 swing-out uprights to length and width (one should be 3/4 in. narrower than the other). Use a countersink bit to predrill holes along one edge, then glue and screw the two edges together. The diagonal measurement (see Photo 7) should be less than the cabinet opening.

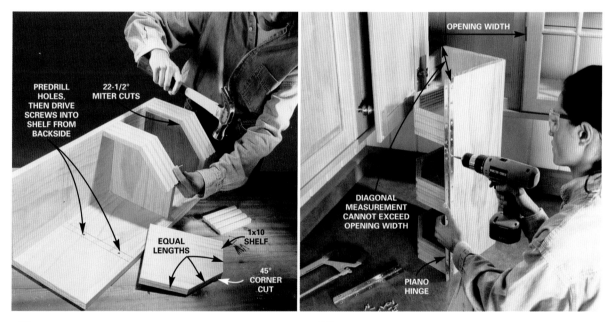

6 Assemble the shelf unit. First mark the shelf positions on the uprights and predrill holes from the front side. Create the three shelves by cutting a 1x10 to length and width, then cutting the corner at 45 degrees. Hold the shelves in place and drive drywall screws through these holes from the backside into the shelves. Cut the 22-1/2-degree angles on the front moldings and secure them with 3d finish nails. You can use any type of wide decorative molding that's at least 1/2 x 3 inches.

7 Screw the piano hinge to the front edge of the swing-out unit, then to the edge of the cabinet face frame. Make certain the swing-out has 1/2 in. of top and bottom clearance. Use an assistant to help you lift and hold the unit at the proper height while you're securing it to the cabinet.

Space-saving cabinet
Built to nest between wall studs

Built into the wall, between the studs, this unobtrusive cabinet extends only 2-1/4 in. into the room. Yet it can hold a small warehouse of supplies—canned goods, cereal, paper towels, six-packs of soda. Or brooms, cleaning products, mops and more. And you can build it in a weekend for about $135.

Install it on an inside wall in the kitchen, bathroom, hallway or on any inside wall where you have drywall and two studs that are 16 in. on-center. The stud cavities must be free of insulation, ductwork, electrical and plumbing lines. Installing the cabinet in a plaster wall, though possible, would be trickier: Cutting plaster straight is difficult, plus you'd need to add a back to the cabinet to cover the rough plaster-and-lath back wall.

The cabinet's case and shelves are made from No. 2 pine 1x6s (actual size: 3/4 x 5-1/2 inches). There's no need to cut these pieces to width, only to length. Doors are cut from 3/4-in. MDF (medium-density fiberboard). MDF is sold by some, but not all, home centers, so call around. Almost any home

project at a glance

skill level
beginner

tools
drill
router
circular saw

cost
about $125–$150

materials list

- 56' No. 2 1x6 pine
- 16' No. 2 1x2 pine
- 4x8 sheet of 3/4" MDF (medium-density fiberboard)
- 56 plug-in shelf supports
- 2 piano hinges, 1-1/2" x 72" long
- 4 magnetic door catches
- 2 door pulls
- 1 tube of paintable caulk
- 1 tube of construction adhesive
- 2" and 1-5/8" No. 6 Phillips head screws
- Small piece of pegboard
- Paint

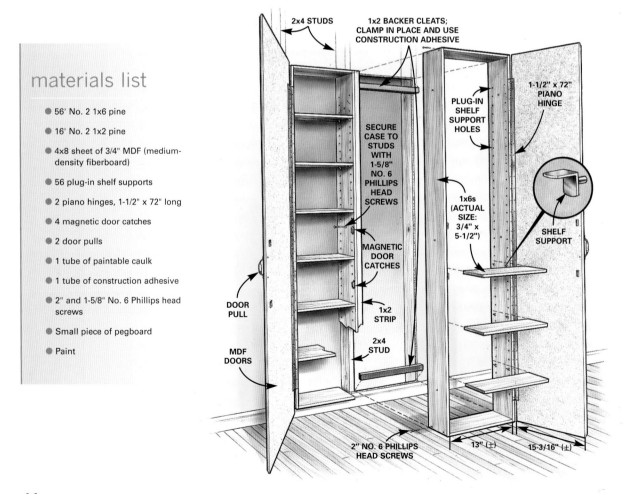

2x4 STUDS

1x2 BACKER CLEATS; CLAMP IN PLACE AND USE CONSTRUCTION ADHESIVE

1-1/2" x 72" PIANO HINGE

PLUG-IN SHELF SUPPORT HOLES

SECURE CASE TO STUDS WITH 1-5/8" NO. 6 PHILLIPS HEAD SCREWS

1x6s (ACTUAL SIZE: 3/4" x 5-1/2")

SHELF SUPPORT

MAGNETIC DOOR CATCHES

DOOR PULL

1x2 STRIP

MDF DOORS

2x4 STUD

2" NO. 6 PHILLIPS HEAD SCREWS

13" (±)

15-3/16" (±)

STUDS

CUT PEEK HOLE FIRST

80"

14-1/2" ±

14-1/2" ±

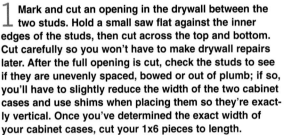

DRILLING GUIDE BLOCK

FRONT EDGE

FRONT

PEG-BOARD

1 Mark and cut an opening in the drywall between the two studs. Hold a small saw flat against the inner edges of the studs, then cut across the top and bottom. Cut carefully so you won't have to make drywall repairs later. After the full opening is cut, check the studs to see if they are unevenly spaced, bowed or out of plumb; if so, you'll have to slightly reduce the width of the two cabinet cases and use shims when placing them so they're exactly vertical. Once you've determined the exact width of your cabinet cases, cut your 1x6 pieces to length.

2 Drill holes for the plug-in shelf supports in the inner 1x6 sides of the case. Use pegboard, clamped in place and aligned with the front edge, to position the holes accurately. Space the holes exactly the same on all four of the sides so your shelves will be level. The drilling guide block, cut from a piece of 2x4, keeps the drill bit exactly vertical (drill the guide hole in the block as straight as possible, aligning it carefully by eye). The block also serves as a stop to prevent the bit from coming through the other side.

center will special-order it if they don't stock it. Using plywood or particleboard for doors this long isn't recommended; both are less stable than MDF and could warp.

The step-by-step photos and descriptions, and the detailed drawing, provide all the information you need to build and install the cabinet. You can paint your cabinet white, both inside and out, or paint it the same color as the walls, so that it's hardly noticeable in the room.

Handy Hints®

Before you begin the main cuts, make a smaller peek hole, just large enough to see that there are no obstructions within the two stud cavities. If the location isn't usable, you can easily patch the small hole.

3 Assemble the two cases with 2-in. No. 6 Phillips head screws. Drill pilot holes, and countersink the screwheads to keep the wood from splitting. No glue is needed.

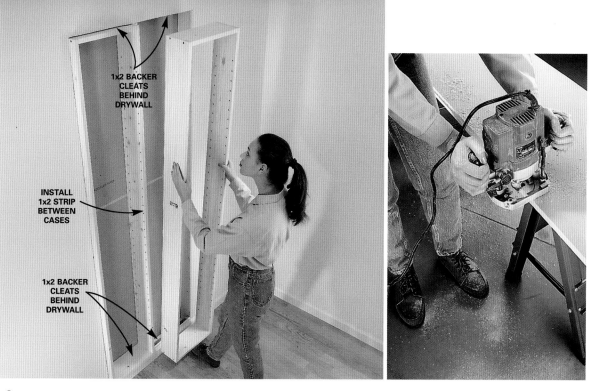

1x2 BACKER CLEATS BEHIND DRYWALL

INSTALL 1x2 STRIP BETWEEN CASES

1x2 BACKER CLEATS BEHIND DRYWALL

4 Mount the two cases in the openings. Use shims if necessary to get the cases level and plumb. Slide a 1x2 strip (the same width as the thickness of the center stud) between the two cases, flush with the leading edge, as shown in the illustration, p. 44. Clamp the strip and cases together, then screw them together. Next, press the back edges of the cases securely against the rear drywall, and secure them to the studs. *NOTE* the 1x2 backer cleats, shown here and in the illustration; they help support the cut drywall edges. Clamp these four cleats in place to the backside of the drywall with construction adhesive and allow the adhesive to dry before installing the cases.

5 Rout finished edges on the doors, after cutting them to size (cut them on a table saw or with a circular saw using a clamped-in-place straight-edge guide). Here, a 1/4-in.-radius cove bit was used in a router to form the edges, but you could use a simple round-over bit. Sand the edges after routing.

6 Hang the doors using 1-1/2-in.-wide x 72-in.-long piano hinges. Getting the doors aligned can be frustrating, but here's a trouble-free method: First, mount both hinges on the case edges flush with the inside edges of the case, using only three screws. Next, set the doors in place, against the closed hinges. TIP: Prop the doors to exactly the right height with a stack of books under each door. Get a uniform 1/16-in. spacing between the two doors. Next, using a fine-tip marker, mark the position of the outside door edge on the exposed barrel of the hinge. Open one door, sliding the supporting books along under it; line up the door edge with the mark on the hinge barrel, then mark two screw-hole locations on the inside of the door, as shown. Predrill small pilot holes, and install the two screws. Do the same with the other door, then check the alignment. Fine-tune the screw positions on the doors if necessary, then install the rest of the screws with a small Phillips head bit in your drill/driver.

MARK SCREW HOLE LOCATIONS IN TWO PLACES

1-1/2" x 72" PIANO HINGE

PROP DOORS TO EXACT HEIGHT WITH STACKED BOOKS

PAINTABLE CAULK

7 Caulk the joint where the drywall and case adjoin, and smooth it with your finger or a small putty knife. After priming and painting the cabinet parts and the back wall, mount the shelf supports and shelves, and install door pulls and magnetic door catches.

Door-mounted spice and lid racks

There's even storage on the back of a door

These simple racks will help transform those chaotic gangs of spice bottles and pan lids into orderly regiments. Here you'll learn how to build only the spice rack; the lid rack uses the same steps but without the shelves. Each spice rack can hold 20 to 30 bottles, and each lid rack two to six lids, depending on the height and width of your cabinet doors. Before building, measure your spice bottles and lids to determine the spacing of your shelves and dowels.

project at a glance

skill level
beginner

tools
drill
jigsaw

cost
under $10

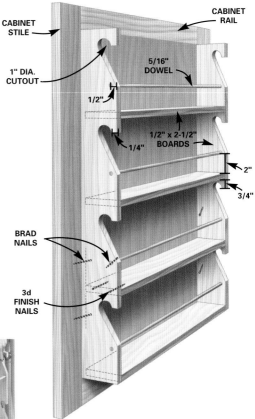

CABINET STILE

CABINET RAIL

1" DIA. CUTOUT

5/16" DOWEL

1/2"

1/4"

1/2" x 2-1/2" BOARDS

2"

3/4"

BRAD NAILS

3d FINISH NAILS

The key measurements and clearances:

Existing shelf depth. If the existing cabinet shelves are full depth, narrow them by about 2 in. to accommodate each door-mounted rack. Shelves that are permanently affixed in grooves in the cabinet sides will need to be cut in place with a jigsaw. Adjustable shelves can be removed, cut along the backside with a circular saw or table saw, then replaced. You may need to move brackets or add holes to remount narrowed shelves.

Spice rack depth and positioning. Make certain the

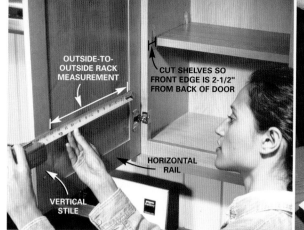

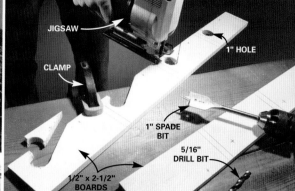

1 Measure the distance between the two vertical stiles and the two horizontal rails to determine the outside dimensions of your spice rack. Cut existing shelves back 2 in. so they don't interfere with the rack when the door is closed.

2 Transfer dimensions from the illustration on p. 48 onto 1/2 x 2-1/2 in. side boards. Cut out the sides of the spice rack. Drill 1-in. holes to create the circular shape, then finish the cutout with a jigsaw. Drill 5/16-in. holes for the dowels. Sand parts smooth.

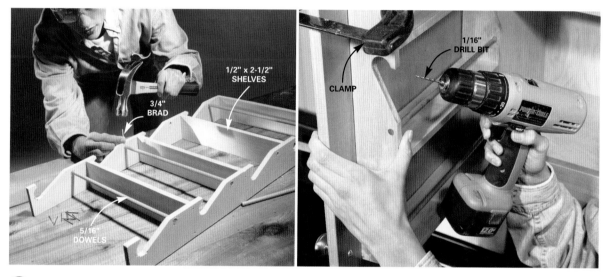

3 Glue and nail the shelves in place one at a time, using 3d finish nails. Then use 3/4-in. brads to pin the dowels in place. Sink all nailheads using a nail set. Apply polyurethane or other finish to match the cabinets.

4 Clamp the finished rack to the door, then drill angled pilot holes through the rack and into the door every 8 inches. Secure with brad nails (remove the door for this step if you find you need a more solid surface for hammering). Use carpenter's glue for a more permanent installation.

new rack won't hit the cabinet frame when the door swings. In this case, fitting the rack between the two 2-in.-wide vertical stiles (Photo 1) provided adequate room. If your doors are solid wood or laminate, hold in place a scrap of wood the same depth as the spice rack (2-1/2 in. was the depth used here) and swing the door. Move it away from the door edge until it no longer makes contact with the cabinet frame, then mark the door. This will determine the overall width of your spice rack.

Use soft, easy-to-nail pine and basswood for both the spice and the lid racks. If you're using a harder wood, like maple or oak, position the pieces, then predrill holes through the side pieces and into the shelf ends. This will prevent splitting and make nailing easier. Install your shelves one at a time so you don't have to balance and juggle multiple pieces as you work. Always nail on a flat, solid surface.

Handy Hints®

Use high-gloss polyurethane for natural wood and high-gloss enamel for painted wood. These finishes are more scrubbable.

Pull-out trash drawer

Here's a better solution for the trash than under the sink—a large waist-high drawer.

Melamine board—particleboard with a tough plastic coating—is a good material for this project because it's easy to clean. A 4x8 sheet costs about $25 at home centers. The Melamine coating, however, tends to chip during cutting. This chipping is worst where the saw teeth exit the material. So with a jigsaw, for example, the face-up side of the sheet will chip.

Plan ahead so the chipped edges are out of view.

You'll also need iron-on edge banding (available at home centers) to cover the exposed edges (Photo 2). When cutting the platform to width, subtract 1/16 in. to allow for the width of the edge banding.

Drawer slides rated for 75- or 100-lb. loads are fine for most drawers. But since this drawer will get more use than most, 120-lb. slides are a good idea (see Resources, p. 186).

If the back of your cabinet door is a flat surface, you can run strips of double-faced tape across the front, stick the door in place and fasten it with four small "L" brackets. The back of the door shown here has a recessed panel, so getting it positioned right was a trial-and-error process. Before removing the door, cut blocks that fit between the door and the floor. Then extend the unit, rest the door on the blocks and attach two brackets. If the resulting fit isn't quite perfect, move the brackets slightly, check again and add the remaining brackets.

project at a glance

skill level
beginner to intermediate

tools
jigsaw
circular saw
drill
iron (for edge banding)

cost
about $50

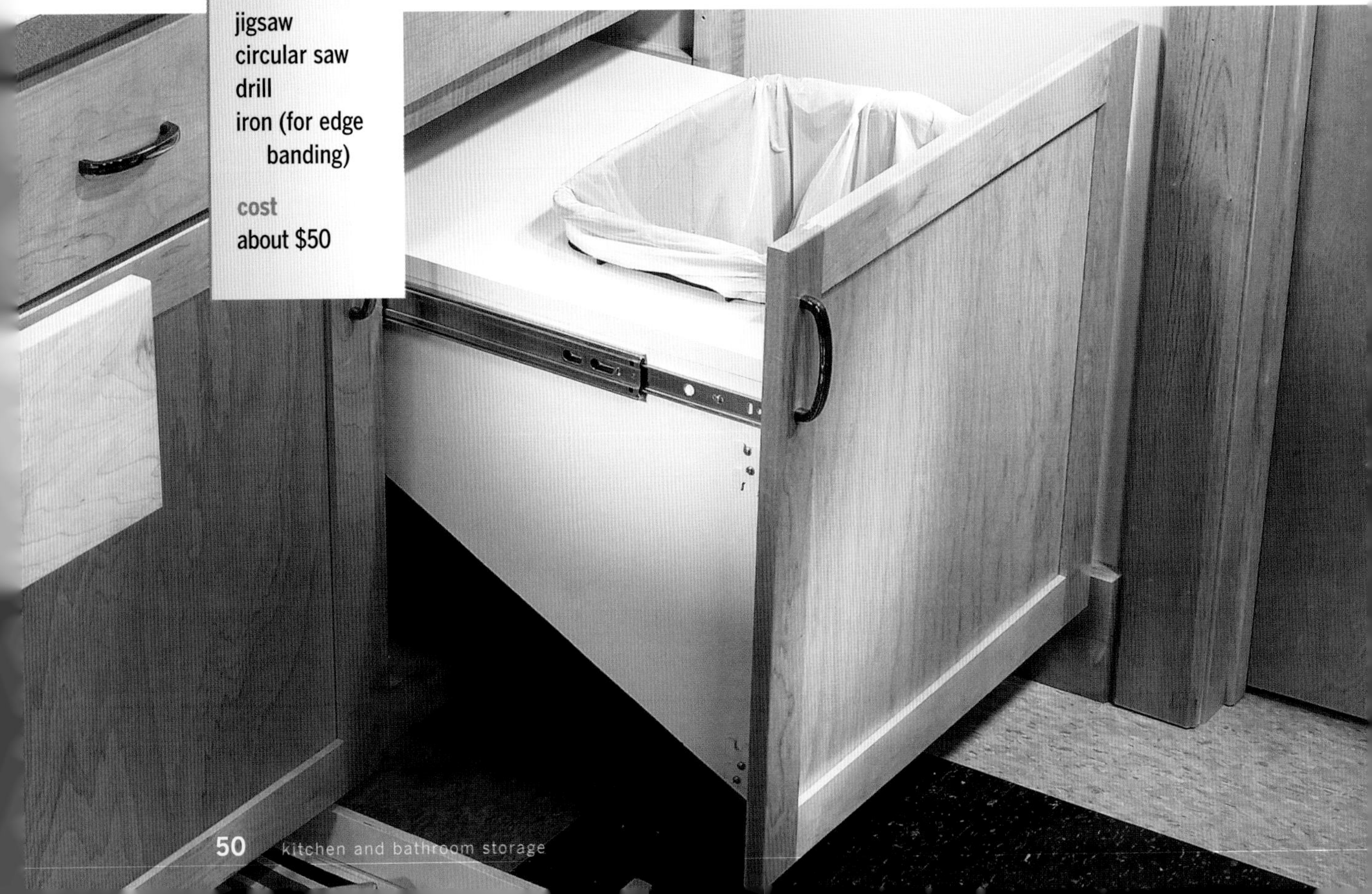

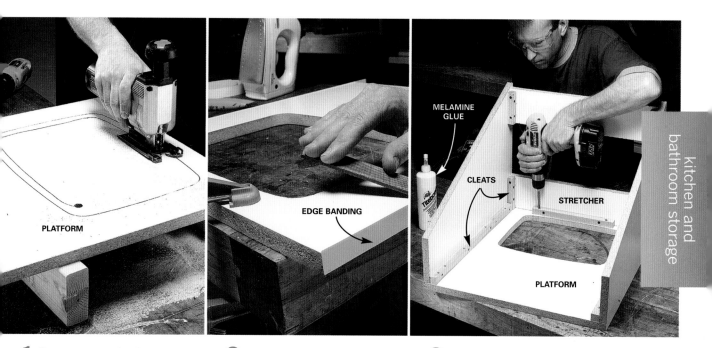

1 Cut out an opening for the trash bin with a jigsaw after placing the bin upside down and tracing around the rim. To allow for the rim, cut about 1/2 in. inside the outline, then check the fit and enlarge the opening as needed.

2 Edge band the Melamine and file away the excess edge banding. To avoid loosening the banding, cut only as you push the file forward, not as you pull back. If you do loosen the edge banding, just reapply with the iron.

3 Assemble the unit with screws and 3/4-in. x 3/4-in. cleats. Be sure to use coarse-threaded screws; fine threads won't hold in particleboard. For extra strength, you can use glue that's made especially for Melamine's slick surface.

personally
speaking

Whoever decreed that the trash can goes under the sink got it wrong. With plumbing in the way, there's no space for a good-size can. Plus who likes to bend over and reach into the cabinet?

Here's a great alternative: In one cabinet, replace the shelves with a simple trash can holder mounted on drawer slides. By attaching the existing cabinet door to the front of the pull-out unit, you create a convenient trash drawer. Here's how to build the unit.

–Gary Wentz, editor
The Family Handyman

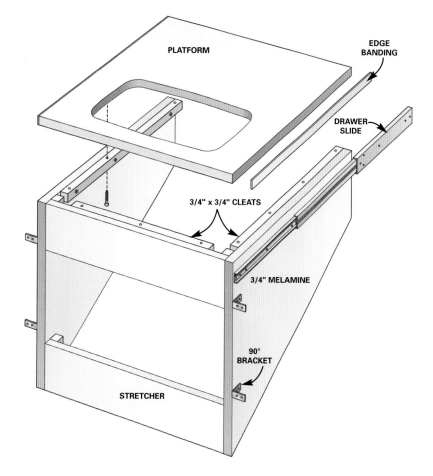

Toe-kick drawers
Make every nook and cranny count

The toe-kick under the cabinets shown here was just a strip of 1/4-in. plywood backed by 5/8-in. particleboard (Photo 1). You might run into something different, like particleboard without any backing at all. In any case, opening up the space under the cabinet is usually fairly easy.

To determine the dimensions of the cradle, measure the depth and width of the space and subtract 1/16 in. from both to provide some adjustment room. If your floor covering is thicker than 1/4 in. (ceramic tile, for example), you may have to glue plywood scraps to the underside of the cradle to raise it and prevent the drawer from scraping against the floor when extended. Size the drawer to allow for slides and the cradle's sides.

Don't worry too much about an exact match of the finish with your existing cabinets. In that dark toe space, nobody will be able to tell. For hardware, consider handles instead of knobs so you can pull the drawers open with your toe.

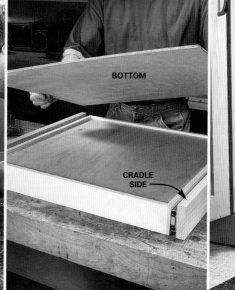

1 Pry off the toe-kick and remove the backing by drilling a large hole near the center, cutting the backing in half and tearing it out. Then grab a flashlight and check for blocks, protruding screws or anything else that might interfere with the drawer.

2 Build a cradle, simply two sides and a bottom, to hold the drawer. Attach the cradle's sides to the slides and drawer, then add the plywood bottom.

3 Slip the cradle under the cabinet. Then drive a pair of screws through each side and into the cabinet box as far back as you can reach.

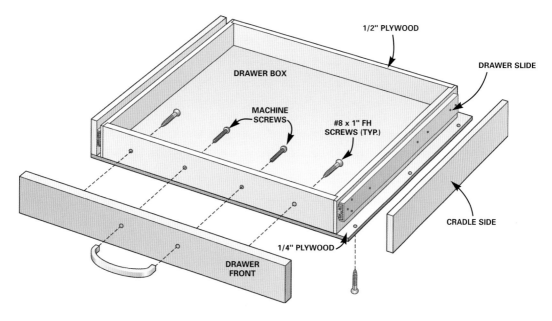

personally speaking

I always looked at the toe space under the cabinets in my too-small kitchen and thought it would be a great place to add drawers. After some head scratching, I found a way to do it without having to install drawer slides in that dark, cramped space. I mounted the drawer and slides in a self-contained cradle that slips easily under the cabinet.

Because the cabinet overhangs the toe-kick by 3 or 4 in., full-extension slides are a necessity for this project. Better yet, use "overtravel" slides that extend an extra inch.

–Gary Wentz, editor
The Family Handyman

Roll-out kitchen trays

At last! Reach that stuff in the back!

These adjustable-height, roll-out trays replace old shelves and work like shallow drawers to give you easy access. You'll love the newfound convenience, and they're especially handy for older or physically challenged people.

This is a project you can easily do in one day for about $45 per base cabinet. Any base cabinet with single or double doors can be modified for roll-out shelving. These photos show you how to install these shelves in a face-frame-style cabinet with double doors *without* a center partition between the doors. The same techniques can be applied to single-door cabinets. Double-door cabinets with a partition should be treated like two single-door cabinets. If you have box or European-style cabinets, you can also use the same techniques shown here.

Tools and skills

Don't be intimidated—this project doesn't require any cabinetmaking skills. If you have any experience with basic carpentry, take it on. The step-by-step instructions and photos show the use of a table saw, but you can do the job with a good circular saw with a rip guide. You'll also need basic tools like a tape measure, hammer and screwdriver.

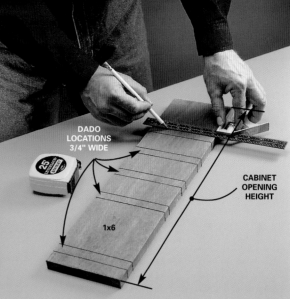

1 Measure the width, height and depth (inside of face frame to back of cabinet) of the cabinet opening. Measure the width with the doors open as shown. The actual finished trays (including sides) will be about 1-1/2 in. less in width and 1 in. less in depth than the opening.

2 Mark 1/4-in.-deep by 3/4-in.-wide dadoes for the vertical supports (see Photo 5). The dadoes hold the horizontal supports and allow you to adjust the height of the roll-out trays.

Getting materials

It's impossible to give exact measurements for your particular cabinet, so here's how to measure to find out what you need.

Begin by measuring the width of the opening between the doors when they are opened straight toward you. The plywood bottom (Photo 6) of each roll-out tray will be about 3 in. narrower than the opening. The depth of the plywood tray bottom will be 2-1/2 in. less than the measured depth (from the back of the cabinet to the back of the face frame). Use these measurements as a guide to buy the appropriate amount of 3/4-in. plywood for the tray bottoms. The tray sides are also made from 3/4-in. plywood; these are cut into 2-1/4-in. strips using the table saw.

You'll also need some 3/4-in.-thick hardwood for the vertical and horizontal supports (Photo 5). It's important to use hardwood for the supports. They have to be able to take the abuse of heavy loads added to the trays.

To help you estimate your materials, here's what you would need for two roll-out trays for a standard 24-in.-wide base cabinet:

- 4 ft. of 1x6 hardwood (oak, birch, maple, cherry, etc.).
- a half sheet of 3/4-in. A-2 plywood (finish grade on both sides), particleboard or Melamine-coated particleboard.
- 22-in. Euro-style epoxy-coated drawer slides (see Resources, p. 186), one pair per tray.
- construction adhesive, carpenter's glue and 6d finish nails.

Follow the step-by-step photos for installation instructions.

Finishing the trays

Remove the drawer slides and sand the entire tray with 100-grit, then 150-grit sandpaper. Follow up with two coats of polyurethane varnish. If you use a Melamine-coated tray bottom, you'll need to sand and varnish only the sides and ends of the tray.

3 Cut the dadoes by making multiple passes on your table saw, or if you have a radial arm saw, use it instead. You can also use a special dado blade. These dadoes should hold the horizontal supports snugly (see Photo 5).

Guard must be removed for this step— use care!

4 Rip the two front vertical supports (3/4 in. wide) from the 1x6 dadoed board first, then rip the wider (1-3/4 in.) back vertical supports. Set them in place in the cabinet.

Guard removed for photo— use yours!

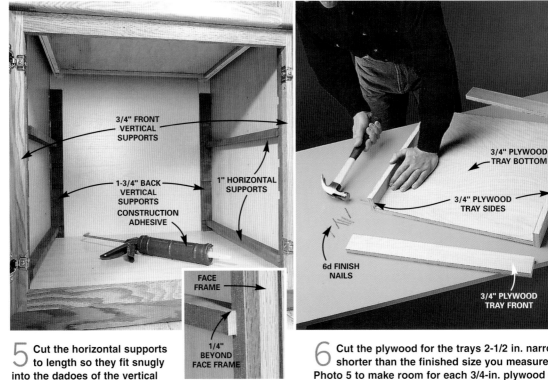

5 Cut the horizontal supports to length so they fit snugly into the dadoes of the vertical supports. The horizontal supports should be ripped wide enough so they project at least 1/4 in. past the face frame. Put a couple of dabs of construction adhesive on the backs of each vertical support, install them permanently as shown, then leave the horizontal supports in place for at least an hour while you make the trays. *Don't glue the horizontal supports.* With the horizontal supports in place, measure the distance between them and make the roll-out trays 1 in. narrower (including tray sides). This allows room for the drawer slides.

6 Cut the plywood for the trays 2-1/2 in. narrower and shorter than the finished size you measured in Photo 5 to make room for each 3/4-in. plywood side and drawer slide. Next, rip the 3/4-in.-thick plywood side and end pieces to 2-1/4 in. and cut them to length. Next, glue and nail the side pieces to the plywood. Finish the trays by gluing and nailing the overlapping end pieces to the front and back.

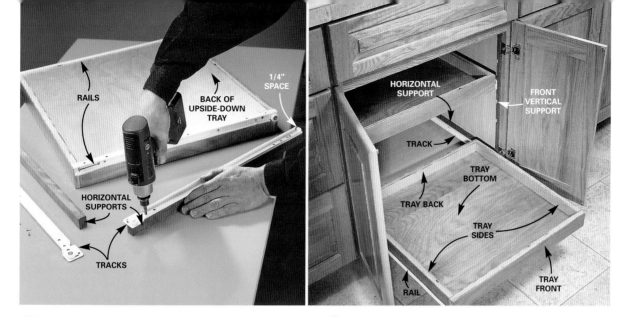

7 Remove the horizontal supports and screw the epoxy-coated slides to each one. The tracks are positioned so that there's 1/4 in. of space at the back of each horizontal support. Flip the finished tray upside-down and screw the epoxy-coated rails to the tray sides. Align the rails flush with the front of the completed tray. Be sure the nylon rollers are toward the back of the tray.

8 Install the horizontal supports and the trays with the rails attached, then check the fit. They should glide easily. If they're hard to move, the trays may be a bit too large. If so, remove the tray and horizontal support and plane the backside of the support until the tray glides effortlessly.

Handy Hints®

Spice up a kitchen drawer

If you need to empty half the spice cupboard just to find the coriander for your curry, this drawer-sized spice rack is the perfect solution. A few scraps of plywood and a little glue are all you need. Lay it in your drawer and all your spice bottles are neatly arranged and visible. It sure is satisfying to find a little project that lets you visit the shop for a couple of hours and come away with a truly useful project.

The dimensions given will work for most drawers, but every drawer is different. Cut a couple test pieces to make sure your spice bottles will fit.

Open kitchen shelves

Converting a few of your wall cabinets to open shelving is a great way to create display space for dishes or to keep cookbooks and cooking supplies within easy reach. Anyone handy with a paintbrush can complete this project in a leisurely weekend. Don't forget to order the glass shelves about a week before you need them.

You'll need a screwdriver, hammer and tape measure as well as basic painting equipment like a paintbrush, putty knife, masking tape and sandpaper or a sanding sponge. Use a drill with a 9/32-in. bit to drill holes for the metal sleeves (Photo 3).

Some cabinets are easy to convert by simply removing the doors and ordering glass shelves. Others may require a little carpentry work, like removing a fixed shelf. Take a close look inside the cabinet to see whether there are hidden challenges. If it looks good, remove the doors and carefully measure for shelves. Measure from one side of the cabinet to the other and from front to back. Deduct 1/8 in. from these meas-

urements to arrive at the glass size. Look in the Yellow Pages under "Glass" to find a company that will cut the glass and polish all of the edges. About $30 was spent for the three 1/4-in.-thick glass shelves in this kitchen. Ask the glass salesperson what thickness you need for strength and safety. Longer spans require thicker glass.

While you're waiting for the glass to arrive, paint the cabinet interiors. Choose a color that matches or complements a floor or wall color. Preparation is the key to a long-lasting, perfectly smooth paint job. Photos 1 and 2 show the painting steps. If you're painting over Melamine or another hard, shiny surface, make sure to thoroughly roughen the surface with 80-grit sandpaper and prime with shellac before brushing or spraying on the coats of paint.

Photo 3 shows the hardware used to support the glass shelves. If you don't have holes for the shelf pins, use a tape measure and square to mark the hole locations and bore 9/32-in. holes to accept the metal reinforcing sleeves.

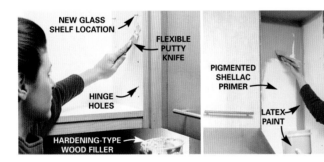

1 Remove the cabinet doors and hinges. Fill all extra shelf bracket or hinge holes with a hardening-type wood filler. Allow this to harden, sand it smooth and apply a coat of lightweight surfacing compound to fill low spots left after the wood filler shrinks. Let the second coat dry. Then sand the entire cabinet interior with 80-grit sandpaper to provide a rough surface for the paint to grab.

2 Use masking tape to protect unpainted areas. Prime the interior with white pigmented shellac (BIN is one brand) to keep the filler from showing through and to provide a binder for the final coats of paint. Sand the primer lightly with a fine sanding sponge after it dries. Remove the dust with a vacuum cleaner and brush on the final coats of latex or oil paint.

3 Support glass shelves with metal shelf pins (see Resources, p. 186) inserted into holes drilled in the cabinet sides. To prevent the pins from enlarging the holes, drill 9/32-in. holes and tap in metal sleeves. Then insert the metal shelf support pins in the sleeves and apply a self-adhesive round rubber pad to each pin to keep the glass shelves from sliding off.

Glass shelves

Most bathrooms have one space you can count on for additional storage, and that's over the toilet. Open glass shelving is a great place to display decorative bathroom bottles or knick-knacks. There are zillions of glass shelving systems on the market. Follow the directions that come with the system for the installation details, but read on for help anchoring them to the wall because you probably won't have studs exactly where you need them. Use masking tape to avoid marking the walls.

1 Apply a strip of 2-in.-wide masking tape above the center of the toilet and on both sides where the shelf brackets will be mounted. Draw a center line with a level and mark the heights of the shelves on the center tape. Transfer the heights to the bracket tape with a 2-ft. level. Then measure from the center line to mark the exact left and right locations for the brackets.

2 Indent the drywall at the marks with a Phillips head screwdriver and remove the tape.

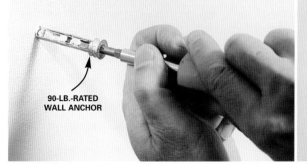

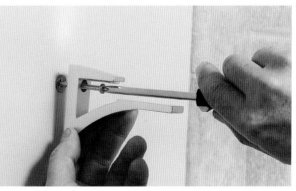

3 Select hollow wall anchors based on wall thickness and weight rating, and install them.

4 Screw the brackets to the wall using the screws included with the anchors.

Gallery of ideas

Cabinet manufacturers, kitchen designers and inventive homeowners are continually coming up with ideas for carving more storage space out of kitchens and cabinets. See Resources on p. 186 for additional information.

Countertop pantry

This mini-pantry with adjustable shelves, door-mounted storage racks and spice drawers provides easily accessed space for those kitchen items you like to keep at your fingertips.

Two-tiered drawer

A sliding top tray takes advantage of otherwise wasted space and helps better organize silverware, cutlery and gadgets.

< **Baskets
and bins**
Slide-out
baskets provide
storage space
without the
hassle of doors.
See-through
bins add a
decorative,
yet functional,
touch to this
island work
area.

Photo courtesy of Plato

< **Recycling
space saver**
Four mid-size
recycling and
trash bins
mounted in a
plywood frame-
work are easy
to access,
remove and
replace thanks
to full-extension
glides.

Photo courtesy of KraftMaid

61

section 3

closet
shelving
systems

Modular closet organizer.........64

Simple closet organizer 70

Handy Hints® 77

Custom-built
    closet organizer.......................78

Gallery of ideas 87

Modular closet organizer

Expert planning advice and step-by-step instructions for making every inch of storage count

If you find yourself rummaging in your closet every morning mumbling to yourself, "One of these days I've got to get organized," then read on, because here's the solution.

For about the price of a dresser, you can install modular closet organizers that practically double your storage space and look great, too. The units are constructed of particleboard with a durable Melamine coating. Although wire shelves are more economical, the modular systems offer several advantages: They look like built-in units, offer adjustable shelves and closet rods, and allow you to add drawers or shelves in the future.

Installing a modular closet system is a great weekend project. The Melamine units shown here assemble easily with special locking hardware. If you're familiar with basic leveling, drilling and sawing, you'll have no problem assembling and installing the units in an average-sized closet in half a day. But don't get too excited yet; first you have to measure and plan the

project at a glance

skill level
beginner

tools
drill
circular saw
level
basic hand tools

cost
about $600

LEVEL

LEVEL LINE

SCREW INTO STUDS

BEVELED CLEAT

SHELF USED AS SPACER

STUD MARK

1 Draw a level line on the back wall of the closet to indicate the bottom of the hanging cleats. Refer to the instructions for the height of this line. Locate the studs along this line and mark the wall.

2 Drill 3/16-in. screw clearance holes through the cleat at the stud locations. Then screw the cleat to the wall with 3-in. pan head screws, leaving them a little loose. Use a shelf to space the cleat from the end wall to allow room for the side panel of the storage unit.

making it fit your budget

The biggest difference among brands is in the quality of the drawer slides, closet poles and mounting system and in the range of unit sizes and available options. Better-quality units also have a more durable surface.

closet, round up the parts, and prepare the old closet for the new shelves.

For this project, you'll need a tape measure, a level, a No. 3 Phillips screwdriver, an electric drill with a No. 2 Phillips bit and 3/16-in. wood and 1/2-in. spade bits, a circular saw with a 140-tooth plywood blade and a hacksaw with a 24-tooth-per-inch blade. An electronic stud finder would be handy, but rapping on the wall with your knuckle or looking for nails in the baseboard are great low-tech methods. Once you find the first stud, the others should be spaced at 16- or 24-in. intervals.

Sketch out a master plan

Start by carefully measuring the closet's width, depth and height. Use graph paper to make scaled drawings of the floor plan and each wall where you plan to hang shelves. Include the width and position of the door on your plan. Let each square equal 6 inches. This allows you to sketch in and try out different storage unit options.

The knock-down storage units are available in standard widths, with 12, 18 and 24 in. being the most common. Depths range from 12 to 18 in. depending on the manufacturer. Some units rest on the floor and reach a height of about 84 in.; others, like the ones shown above, hang from a cleat or are rail-mounted to the wall.

Each storage unit consists of two side panels drilled for shelf pins and connecting bolts, one or two hanging cleats and some fixed shelves (Photo 4). The parts are connected with ingenious two-part knock-down fasteners consisting of a connecting bolt that screws into the side panels and a cam mechanism mounted in each fixed shelf and cleat. To assemble, just screw the connecting bolts in the right holes, slide the parts together, and turn the cam clockwise to lock the parts together. There are systems available at home centers and discount stores that simply screw together, but they're harder to assemble and not nearly as sturdy.

The basic units are essentially boxes with a lot of holes

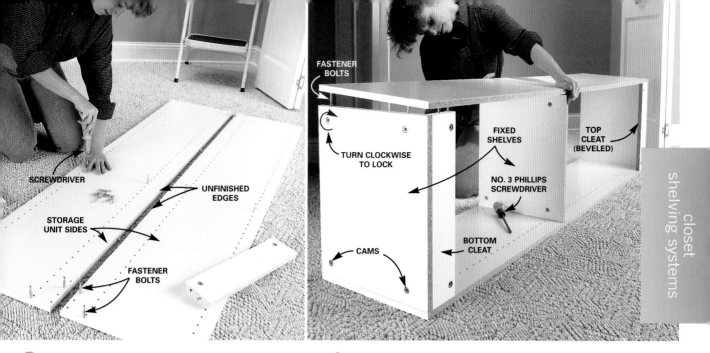

3 Lay the sides of the first storage unit on a carpet or dropcloth with unfinished edges together. Screw fastener bolts for the fixed shelves and cleats into the predrilled holes. Your instruction sheet will show which holes to use.

4 Assemble the cabinet by aligning the holes in the fixed shelves and cleats with the fastener bolts. Lock them together by turning the cams clockwise. Then position the second side and lock it in. Face the cams where they'll be least visible when the cabinet is hung.

drilled in the sides. Complete the system by adding adjustable shelves, drawers and closet rods. All the components are designed to fit into or attach to the predrilled holes, so very little additional drilling is required.

Check the Yellow Pages under "Closet Accessories" and make a few calls to see who sells modular closet systems in your area, or use the Internet to locate local suppliers. Some closet specialists insist on installing the systems, while others will help with the design and provide the storage units, hardware and instructions you need to do your own installation. Take your sketch along and get estimates on a couple of different systems.

The closet system shown above cost about $600. You could save about $150 by using standard-sized, floor-standing, modular storage units, but that would require settling for a less efficient plan and doing more assembly work. Also, hanging the units on the wall avoids the extra work of cutting around or removing baseboards or dealing with uneven floors and keeps your floor clear for cleaning.

Although Melamine-coated shelving is a great product for an affordable, prefinished storage unit, it does have some limitations. The particleboard core will not stand up to moisture. Wire shelving may be a better choice in damp places. The Melamine coating is more durable than paint but not as tough as the plastic laminate used on countertops, so don't expect this stuff to tolerate the same abuse you give your kitchen counters. Storing books or heavy objects may cause the particleboard to sag over time; consider a stronger material like plywood or metal shelves.

Get your closet ready to go

If your closet is anything like the one shown above, the biggest part of this project will be clearing it out. When that's done, remove the rod, shelf and everything except the baseboard from the walls. Place a scrap of wood under your hammer or pry bar to avoid crushing the drywall or plaster when you pry off the shelf support boards. Patch the holes with a lightweight surfacing compound. Then sand and repaint the walls and you're ready to hang shelves.

Once your design is complete and the closet walls are patched and painted, it's all coasting downhill. The storage unit systems are so well engineered that even if you can't pound a nail, you'll feel like a master cabinetmaker when you're done. Photos 1 through 10 show the basic steps involved. Consult the instruction sheet provided

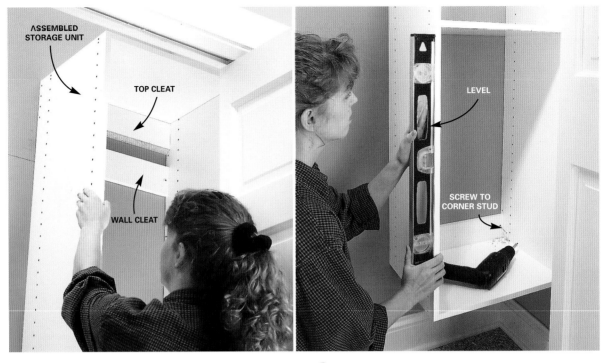

5 Hang the storage unit by pushing it tight to the wall and sliding it down onto the interlocking cleat.

6 Check the side panel to make sure the cabinet is plumb and screw through the bottom cleat into a stud to secure it.

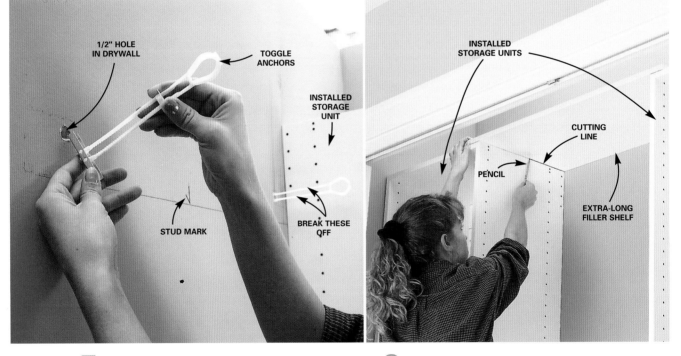

7 Install toggle anchors for additional support if cleats land on only one stud. Hold the cleat in position and drill a 3/16-in. hole through the cleat and the drywall or plaster to mark the location of the toggle anchor. Remove the cleat and enlarge the hole in the wall to 1/2 inch. Then install the anchor and attach the cleat, making sure to leave a space for the side panel of the next storage unit.

8 Mark the oversized filler shelf for cutting by laying it on top of the storage units and drawing lines along each side panel onto the shelf.

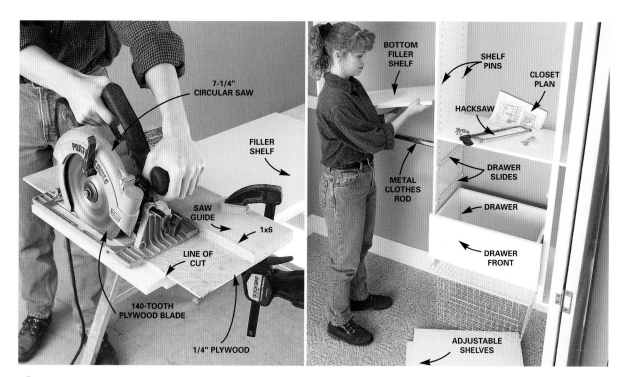

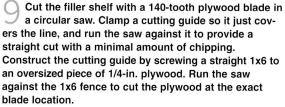

9 Cut the filler shelf with a 140-tooth plywood blade in a circular saw. Clamp a cutting guide so it just covers the line, and run the saw against it to provide a straight cut with a minimal amount of chipping. Construct the cutting guide by screwing a straight 1x6 to an oversized piece of 1/4-in. plywood. Run the saw against the 1x6 fence to cut the plywood at the exact blade location.

10 Tilt in the filler shelves, resting them on shelf support pins. Cut the metal closet rods with a 24-tooth-per-inch hacksaw. Tighten all of the mounting screws after adjacent units are connected. Install drawers, drawer fronts and adjustable shelves.

with your system for exact procedures and placement of connecting bolts and other hardware.

Here are a few assembly tips and things to watch out for:

● Take off the closet doors if they're in your way during construction.

● Extend the level line (Photo 1) only as far as necessary to line up the cleats. Find the studs and mark them above the line, where the marks will be hidden by the cleats. Double-check the stud locations by probing with a nail to be certain the hanging screws will hit solid wood.

● Get help setting the units in place. Avoid twisting the assembled storage units out of shape; the thin area of particleboard near the connectors might break.

Handy Hints®

Check the end walls of your closet with a level to see if they're plumb. If they slant inward on the bottom, you'll have to mount the first cleat farther from the wall to allow the storage unit to hang plumb.

● Don't tighten the mounting screws until you've joined the units with the special two-part connectors. You'll need the "slack" to align the holes properly. If the closet walls are wavy or crooked, slide shims behind the units to get them lined up.

● Install all of the full-size units. Then cut the filler shelves to complete the system (Photos 8 and 9). Tilt the top filler shelf in from below, and then install the shelf clips under it. A snug-fitting shelf is hard to install from the top.

● Some systems have adjustable drawer fronts. Loosen the screws just enough to move the fronts into alignment, with even spacing between the drawers. Then tighten the screws and drill for the knobs.

Simple closet organizer

You get easy-access shoe storage, a set of clothes cubbies and an extra-wide top shelf from only one sheet of plywood

Most bedroom closets suffer from bare minimum organization—stuff on the floor, a long, overloaded closet rod, and a precariously stacked, sagging shelf. You don't have to put up with it. This simple shelving system was designed to clean up some of that clutter. It provides a home for shoes, several cubbies for loose clothing, folded shirts, sweaters or small items, and a deeper (16-in.-wide) top shelf to house the stuff that keeps falling off the narrow shelf. Besides the storage space it provides, the center tower stiffens the shelf above it as well as the clothes rod, since you use two shorter rods rather than one long one.

Here you'll learn how to cut and assemble this shelving system from a single sheet of plywood for a 6-ft.-long closet, including how to mount drawer slides for the shoe trays. Birch plywood is recommended because it's relatively inexpensive (about $35 to $40 per 4 x 8-ft. sheet) yet takes a nice finish. Face the edges with 1x2 maple for strength and a more attractive appearance. The materials for this project are available at most home centers or well-stocked lumberyards.

The key tool for this project is a circular saw with a cutting guide for cutting the plywood into nice straight pieces (Photo 1). An air-powered brad nailer or finish nailer makes the assembly go much faster, and a miter saw helps produce clean cuts. But neither is absolutely necessary. If you're handy with a circular saw, you can cut and assemble this project in about a day. But allow another four hours or so for sanding and finishing the maple plywood and boards.

Cut the birch plywood to size

First, rip the plywood into three 15-3/4-in. by 8-ft. pieces (Photo 1), then cut the sides and shelves from these with a shorter cutting guide. For an average-size closet—6 ft. wide with a 5-1/2 ft. high top shelf—you can cut all the sides and shelves from one piece of 3/4-in. plywood. If you make the shelving wider, you'll have to settle for fewer shelves/trays or buy additional plywood. Be sure to support the plywood so the pieces won't fall after you complete a cut, and use a guide to keep the cuts perfectly straight. Make your cutting guides (a long and a short one) from the factory edges of 1/2-in. particleboard. Use a plywood blade in your circular saw to minimize splintering. Cut slowly on the crosscuts, and make sure the good side of the plywood is down—the plywood blade makes a big difference, but the thin veneer will splinter if you rush the cut.

Mark and cut the baseboard profile on the plywood sides, using a profile gauge (about $8; Photo 2) or a trim scrap to transfer the shape. If you can remove the baseboard easily, you could cut it rather than the plywood and reinstall it later. Either method works fine.

Attach the maple edges

Glue and nail the side 1x2s (G, Figure A, p. 73) to the best-looking side of the plywood (so it faces out), holding them flush with the front edge (Photo 3). Be sure to use 1-1/4-in. brads here so you don't nail completely through the side. You can use 1-1/2-in. brads everywhere else.

1/2" PARTICLE-
BOARD GUIDE

A

A

B

E

E

C

2x4 SUPPORTS

D

E

D

BEST SIDE
FACING DOWN

1 Cut the sheet of plywood into three equal widths
using a saw guide. Then crosscut the sections into
the pieces shown in Figure A, using a shorter guide.

2 Make an outline of the baseboard with a profile
gauge (right) and, using a jigsaw, cut out the pattern
on the lower backside of the two shelving sides. (See A
in Figure A and Photo 4.)

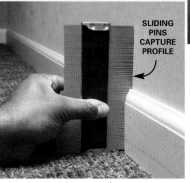

SLIDING
PINS
CAPTURE
PROFILE

Then attach the front 1x2s (F). These 1x2s should be flush with the bottom of the sides, but 3/4 in. short of the top. The 1x2s will overlap the edge slightly because 3/4-in. plywood is slightly less than a full 3/4 in. thick. Keep the overlap to the inside.

Lay out the locations for the drawer slides and the fixed center shelf before assembling the cabinet—the 12-in. width is a tight fit for a drill. Use the dimensions in Photo 4 and Figure A for spacing. You can vary any of these measurements to better fit your shoes or other items you want to store. Then take the drawer slides apart and mount them on the tower sides (Photo 4). Remember that one side of each pair is a mirror image of the other.

To position the shelf support pins for the two adjustable shelves, align the bottom of the 1/4-in. peg board with the fixed shelf location, then drill mirror-image holes on the two sides (Photo 5). Mark the holes that you intend to use on the peg board—it's all too easy to lose track when you flip the peg board over to the second side. Use a brad point drill bit to prevent splintering, and place a bit stop or a piece of tape for a 5/8-in. hole depth (1/4-in. peg board plus 3/8 in. deep in the plywood). Most support pins require a 1/4-in.-diameter hole, but measure to make sure.

Cut the bevels and assemble the shelves

Cut the bevels in all the 1x2 shelf fronts, then glue and nail them to the plywood shelves, keeping the bottoms flush (Photo 6). Nail 1x2 backs (J1 and J2) onto the adjustable and rollout shelves. Next, nail together the bracing (L) and the base piece (K), which join the cabinet. Now add the slides to the rollout shelves (Photo 7).

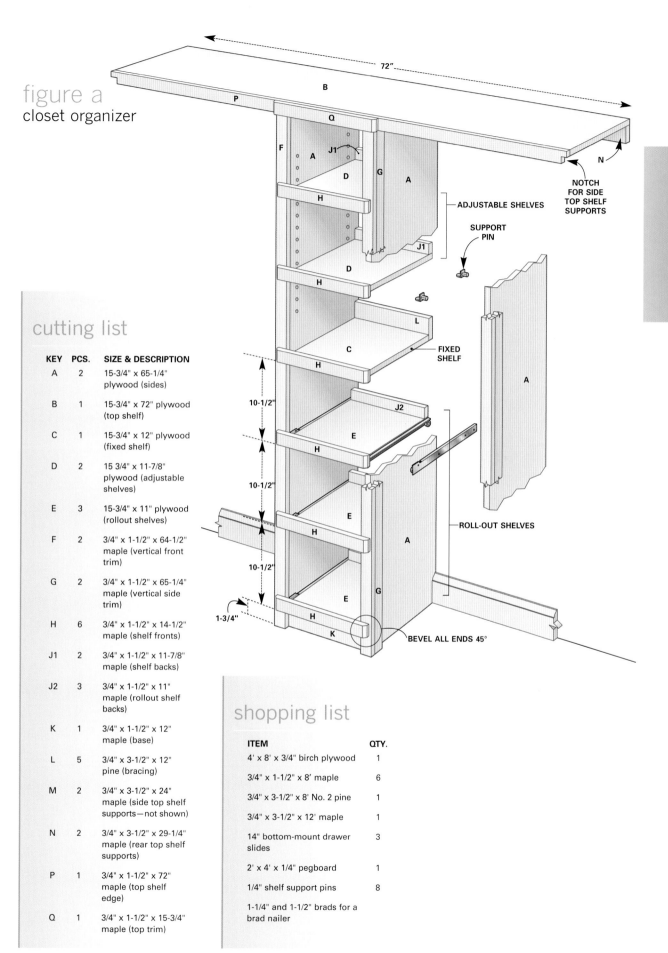

figure a
closet organizer

72"

B

P

Q

F
A
J1
D
G
A

ADJUSTABLE SHELVES

N

NOTCH
FOR SIDE
TOP SHELF
SUPPORTS

SUPPORT
PIN

H

D

H

J1

L

C

FIXED
SHELF

H

A

J2

E

H

10-1/2"

ROLL-OUT SHELVES

E

H

A

10-1/2"

E

H

G

E

10-1/2"

H

K

1-3/4"

BEVEL ALL ENDS 45°

cutting list

KEY	PCS.	SIZE & DESCRIPTION
A	2	15-3/4" x 65-1/4" plywood (sides)
B	1	15-3/4" x 72" plywood (top shelf)
C	1	15-3/4" x 12" plywood (fixed shelf)
D	2	15 3/4" x 11-7/8" plywood (adjustable shelves)
E	3	15-3/4" x 11" plywood (rollout shelves)
F	2	3/4" x 1-1/2" x 64-1/2" maple (vertical front trim)
G	2	3/4" x 1-1/2" x 65-1/4" maple (vertical side trim)
H	6	3/4" x 1-1/2" x 14-1/2" maple (shelf fronts)
J1	2	3/4" x 1-1/2" x 11-7/8" maple (shelf backs)
J2	3	3/4" x 1-1/2" x 11" maple (rollout shelf backs)
K	1	3/4" x 1-1/2" x 12" maple (base)
L	5	3/4" x 3-1/2" x 12" pine (bracing)
M	2	3/4" x 3-1/2" x 24" maple (side top shelf supports—not shown)
N	2	3/4" x 3-1/2" x 29-1/4" maple (rear top shelf supports)
P	1	3/4" x 1-1/2" x 72" maple (top shelf edge)
Q	1	3/4" x 1-1/2" x 15-3/4" maple (top trim)

shopping list

ITEM	QTY.
4' x 8' x 3/4" birch plywood	1
3/4" x 1-1/2" x 8' maple	6
3/4" x 3-1/2" x 8' No. 2 pine	1
3/4" x 3-1/2" x 12' maple	1
14" bottom-mount drawer slides	3
2' x 4' x 1/4" pegboard	1
1/4" shelf support pins	8
1-1/4" and 1-1/2" brads for a brad nailer	

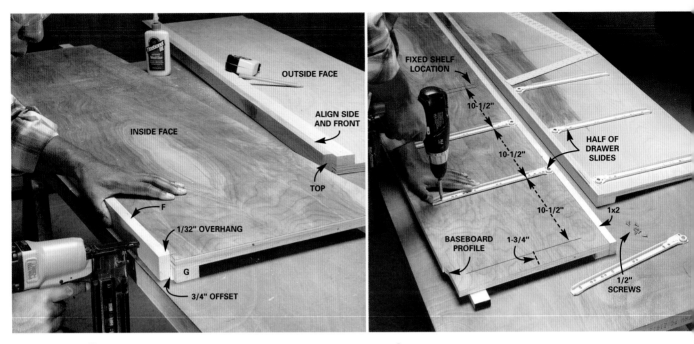

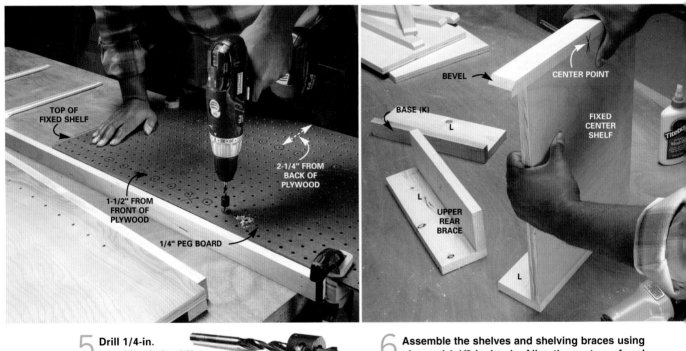

3 Cut the 1x2s to length. Then glue and nail them to the plywood sides (Figure A) with 1-1/4-in. brads. Note the slight (1/32-in.) overhang along the inside.

4 Mark the center and rollout shelf locations using a framing square. Then mount half of each of the two-piece drawer slides even with the 1x2 on each side.

5 Drill 1/4-in. matching holes 3/8 in. deep for the adjustable shelf pins using a peg board template. Flip the peg board when switching sides.

6 Assemble the shelves and shelving braces using glue and 1-1/2-in. brads. Align the centers of each piece for accurate positioning.

7 Attach the other halves of the slides to the rollout shelves with 1/2-in. screws. Butt them against the front 1x2.

8 Set the sides on edge, glue and clamp the braces (L) in place and nail the assembly together with 1-1/2-in. brads. Make sure the braces are square to the sides.

Assembling the shelving tower is straight-forward (Photo 8). Position the L-shaped bracing at the top and braces at the bottom, add glue to the joints, then clamp and nail. Because of the slight lip where the 1x2 front trim (F) overlaps the plywood, you'll have to chisel out a 1/32-in.-deep x 3/4-in.-wide notch so the fixed shelf will fit tightly (Photo 9).

Set the cabinet in the closet

Remove the old closet shelving and position the new cabinet (center it, if possible). If you have carpeting, it's best to cut it out under the cabinet for easier carpet replacement in the future (Photo 10). For the cleanest look, pull the carpet back from the closet wall, cut out the padding and tack strip that fall under the cabinet, and nail new tack strips around the cabinet position. Then reposition the cabinet, push the carpet back against it and cut the carpet.

Or, if you're not fussy about appearance inside the closet, simply cut out the carpet and tack strip under

Handy Hints

Hold your brad nailer perpendicular to the grain whenever possible so the rectangular nail heads will run with the grain instead of cutting across it. This makes them less prominent.

the cabinet and tack the loose carpet edges to the floor.

Plumb and level the cabinet, then screw it to the wall. Use hollow wall anchors if you can't find the studs. The cabinet will be firmly anchored by the upper shelf anyway.

Scribe both ends of the top shelf for a tight fit

Closet shelves are tough to fit because the corners of the walls are rarely square. To cut the shelf accurately, scribe a leftover 16-in.-wide piece of particleboard or plywood in both corners (Photo 11) and use it for a template for cutting the ends of the shelf. Then the shelf will drop right into place and rest on 1x4 supports nailed to the side walls and back wall. Make sure the front of the shelf is flush with the front of the tower and nail it to the top. If the back wall is wavy, you may have to scribe the back of the shelf to the wall and trim it to make the front flush. Then cut and notch the front 1x2 and nail it to the shelf (Photo 12).

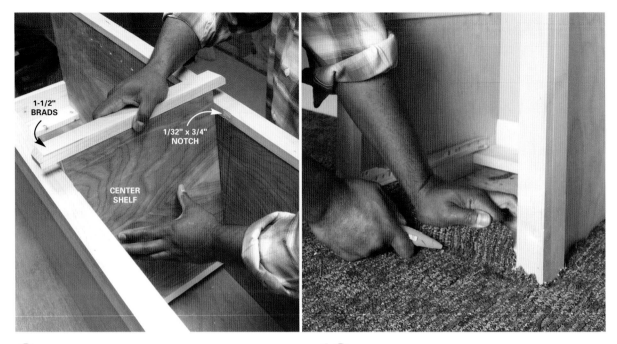

9 Chisel shallow slots in the 1x2 overhang, then slide the center shelf into place. Nail at the front, back and sides.

10 Center the cabinet in the closet against the back wall, mark its position and cut out the carpet around it. Tack the loose edges of carpet to the floor.

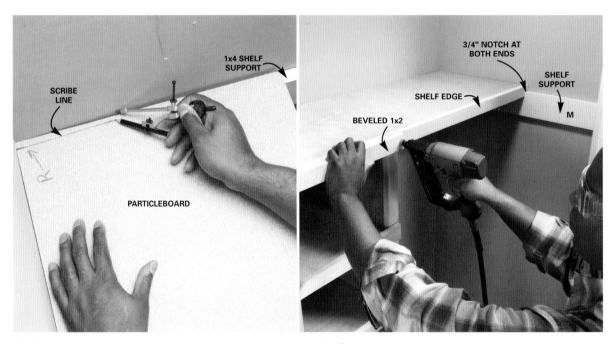

11 Shove a 16 x 24-in. sheet of particleboard into the shelf corners and scribe the angles. Cut the angles and use them as a pattern to trim the shelf. Nail the shelf to the supports and cabinet top.

12 Notch the 1x2 shelf edge over the end supports and nail it into place. Then trim the top of the cabinet with a beveled 1x2.

Lightly sand all the wood and apply a clear finish. When it's dry, mix several shades of putty to get an exact match to your wood and fill the nail holes. Add another coat of finish and let it dry. Screw on the closet rod brackets, aligning them with the bottom of the 1x4. Then pile on the clothes!

Compact storage
for comforters

Billowy comforters, pillows and blankets take up lots of storage space in your closet. To save space, toss those puffy items into a heavy-duty (2-mil or thicker is best) plastic bag. Then use your shop vacuum to remove as much air as possible before tying off the bag.

To keep the items fresh in storage, toss in a fabric softener sheet before you use the vacuum.

HEAVY-DUTY
GARBAGE BAG

Revive an aromatic
cedar closet

Everyone likes the woodsy smell of a new aromatic cedar closet. But the fragrance diminishes once the cedar oils evaporate and dust clogs the wood pores. You can revive much of the aroma by sanding and cleaning the paneling.

Start by emptying the closet, laying down floor protection and draping the area with plastic sheeting to control the sanding dust.

For the best results, use 100-grit sandpaper and move the sander in overlapping side-to-side strokes. Clean the paneling by vacuuming and then wiping it with tack cloths (about $1 each). Avoid using a damp cloth or sponge to remove the cedar dust. Wet-cleaning may raise the wood grain and leave a rough surface and water stains.

ORBITAL SANDER
WITH 100-GRIT
SANDPAPER

Custom-built closet organizer

Double your closet capacity with smart and efficient built-ins, shelving and rod space

s your closet too small and overstuffed? Do your cluttered shelves, packed and sagging clothes rods, and jumbled shoes all cry out for more space? Of course, the coolest solution would be to expand the existing closet, but that's usually impossible. Instead, you can organize your existing closet to make every cubic inch count and get more dresser space to boot.

It's surprisingly easy and economical to squeeze more storage out of limited space. Here you'll learn how to remodel a standard 8-ft.-long, 30-in.-deep closet, a size that's found in millions of homes. Here's what you can do to maximize storage.

● **Cabinet module:** The 2-ft.-wide, 23-in.-deep, 78-in.- tall cabinet module is designed to provide extra drawer and shelving space. The unit is mounted 6 in. above the floor for easy cleaning. The mounting height also makes installation easier because you don't have to fool with removing and reinstalling carpeting or baseboards.

project at a glance

skill level
intermediate to advanced

tools
circular saw
screw gun
carpenter's square
bar clamps
edge banding trimmer

cost
about $300

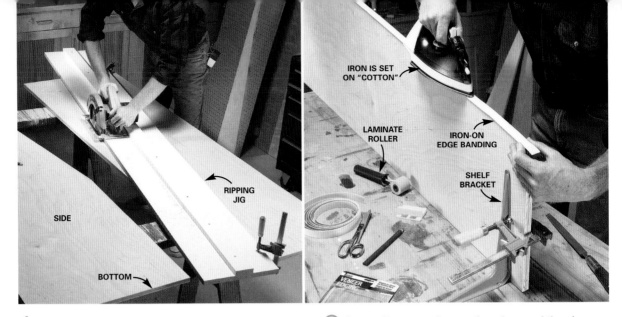

1 Cut the sides to length and width using a ripping jig. Rip the drawer dividers to width only. Cut the angles on the front edge of each cabinet side.

2 Clean off any sawdust on the edges and then iron the edge banding onto the outside edges of the sides and the two lengths of drawer divider stock.

● **Clothes rods:** Rod capacity is maximized because the rods are double-stacked at one end of the closet for shorter clothes like shirts and skirts. The single rod at the other end of the closet is for slacks and dresses.

● **Shoe shelves:** To tame shoe scatter, we've designed a two-tier shoe shelf. Including the space under the shelves, you'll have nine luxurious feet of shoe storage—enough for even those beat-up, knockabout shoes you can't bear to throw out.

Custom-build your own closet system

It's easy to upgrade the typical single rod and shelf found in standard closets for more efficient "closetry." Home centers offer several lines of mix-and-match closet cabinets and organizers so you can design and install a custom closet system. Those systems look inexpensive—until you start adding up all the parts! A similar-size Melamine cabinet module alone will cost about $300. We offer a more handsome, lower-cost alternative—custom-building your own. For that same $300, you'll have a closet full of cabinetry that's so doggone good-looking that you'll want to leave the closet doors open.

This project doesn't call for any fancy woodworking joints. All the parts are end-cut and simply screwed together. While that makes for easy construction, it means you'll have to use plywood-core, veneered plywood

because it'll hold screws and has a smooth, even surface ready for finishing. If you want to use particleboard-core sheets, plan on joining parts with biscuits, dowels or any other fastening system that is familiar to you. Birch plywood was used here to match the bedroom's existing woodwork. All of the materials shown are found at any well-stocked home center.

As for tools, you don't need much aside from a good circular saw, a screw gun, a carpenter's square and two 30-in. bar clamps. You'll also have to blow the dust off the clothes iron and use it to apply the edge banding (Photo 2). But there are a few other optional tools

materials list

ITEM	QTY.
3/4" plywood	3 sheets
1/2" plywood (buy a 4x4 sheet if it's available)	1 sheet
1/4" plywood	1 sheet
Iron-on edge banding	3 rolls
Construction adhesive	1 tube
Woodworking glue	
8' chrome closet rods	1
6' chrome closet rods	1
Closet rod end brackets	3 sets
No. 8 finish washers	50
No. 8 2" oval head screws	40
No. 8 3" oval head screws	12
22" "Liberty" bottom-mount drawer slides	4 sets
Drawer pulls	4 (or 8)
Shelf brackets	12

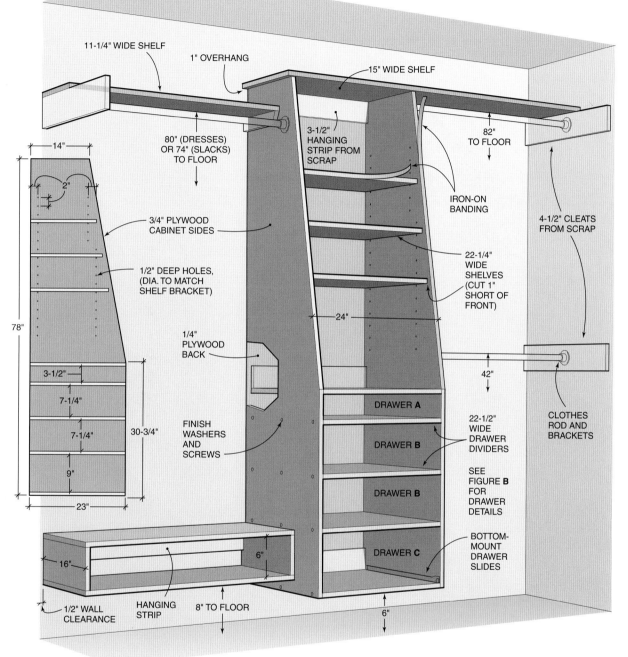

11-1/4" WIDE SHELF

1" OVERHANG

15" WIDE SHELF

3-1/2" HANGING STRIP FROM SCRAP

82" TO FLOOR

80" (DRESSES) OR 74" (SLACKS) TO FLOOR

IRON-ON BANDING

3/4" PLYWOOD CABINET SIDES

4-1/2" CLEATS FROM SCRAP

2"

1/2" DEEP HOLES, (DIA. TO MATCH SHELF BRACKET)

22-1/4" WIDE SHELVES (CUT 1" SHORT OF FRONT)

14"

24"

78"

1/4" PLYWOOD BACK

42"

3-1/2"

7-1/4"

DRAWER A

7-1/4"

DRAWER B

22-1/2" WIDE DRAWER DIVIDERS

CLOTHES ROD AND BRACKETS

30-3/4"

FINISH WASHERS AND SCREWS

DRAWER B

SEE FIGURE B FOR DRAWER DETAILS

9"

23"

DRAWER C

BOTTOM-MOUNT DRAWER SLIDES

16"

6"

1/2" WALL CLEARANCE

HANGING STRIP

8" TO FLOOR

6"

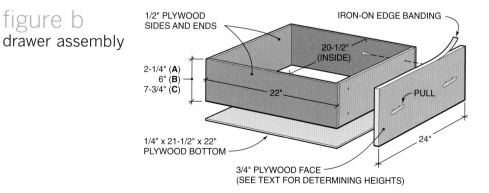

figure b
drawer assembly

1/2" PLYWOOD SIDES AND ENDS

IRON-ON EDGE BANDING

20-1/2" (INSIDE)

2-1/4" (A)
6" (B)
7-3/4" (C)

22"

PULL

1/4" x 21-1/2" x 22" PLYWOOD BOTTOM

24"

3/4" PLYWOOD FACE (SEE TEXT FOR DETERMINING HEIGHTS)

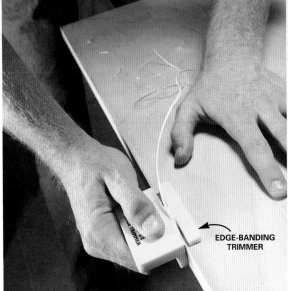

3 Trim the overhanging edges of the edge banding with a trimming tool, then file and sand the edges smooth and flush with the edge.

EDGE-BANDING TRIMMER

4 Mark the shelf bracket hole locations on peg board and use it as a drilling template. Flip the peg board to drill the other side.

30-3/4"

6"

DRILL STOP

LEFT SIDE

RIGHT SIDE

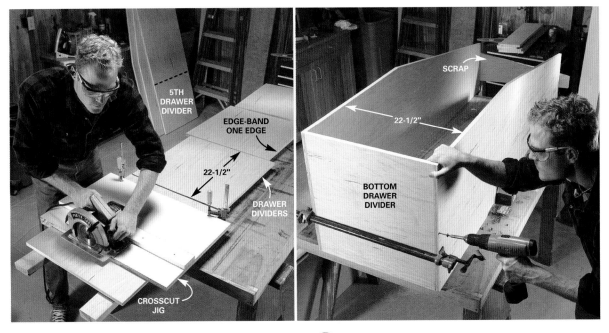

5TH DRAWER DIVIDER

EDGE-BAND ONE EDGE

22-1/2"

DRAWER DIVIDERS

CROSSCUT JIG

SCRAP

22-1/2"

BOTTOM DRAWER DIVIDER

5 Cut the five edge-banded drawer dividers to length with the crosscutting jig, four from one length and one from the other.

6 Screw a scrap to the top of the cabinet, spacing the sides 22-1/2 in. apart, then clamp the bottom drawer divider between the sides. Predrill and fasten.

you'll find useful. While it is possible to hand-nail the parts together, a brad nailer (Photo 8) will speed up construction. (Since you can now buy a brad nailer for less than $100, this project is a good excuse to add it to your tool collection.) Also pick up an edge-banding trimmer for quick, accurate edge trimming (less than $10; Photo 3).

NO. 8 FINISH WASHER

2" NO. 8 OVAL HEAD SCREW

Building the cabinet box

Start the project by cutting the cabinet box sides and two 23-in.-wide lengths for the drawer dividers; see Photos 1 and 5. Consult Figure A, p. 81, for all of the cutting dimensions. Before you cut the drawer dividers to length, edge-band one edge. That way the exposed edges will be finished before they're cut to length.

7 Stand the cabinet upright and rip spacer blocks from scrap to space and support the other drawer dividers as you screw them into place.

8 Glue and pin the cabinet back to the sides and dividers to square the cabinet. Then glue and pin the hanging strips to the back and sides.

9 Glue and pin the drawer sides together with 1-in. brads. Before the glue sets, square each drawer by gluing and pinning the bottom in place.

10 Screw the drawer slides into the cabinet and bottom edges of the drawer boxes. Slide each drawer into place to check the fit.

Before you assemble the cabinet, drill the holes for the adjustable shelving. The old trick of using a peg board jig for consistent hole spacing is used here (Photo 4). Because the sides taper, you'll have to shift over a row or two of holes to keep the narrower top shelf brackets within a few inches of the front. Try to keep the front and rear holes about 2 in. from the edge. Buy a drill bit that matches the shaft on the shelving brackets that you

chose. It's best to use a "brad point" drill bit to prevent splintering the veneer. Either use a depth stop or mark the drill bit with a piece of tape to keep from drilling through the plywood.

Begin assembling the cabinet on its back by attaching a spacer strip at the top and then screwing the bottom drawer divider into place (Photo 6). Predrill with a 1/8-in. bit and drive 2-in.-long No. 8 oval head screws with finish

11 Set the drawer front panel (edge-banded on three sides) on a cleat screwed to the cabinet bottom. Mark and cut lowest drawer front. Edge-band raw edges.

12 Space each panel two quarter coin thicknesses apart, then measure and cut the next. Edge-band the two raw edges that meet, then repeat the procedure.

13 Place crumpled newspaper behind each drawer and replace the drawers. They should stick out about 1/2 in. beyond the cabinet front.

14 Apply four beads of construction adhesive to the drawer boxes and restack the drawer fronts, spacing them with a pair of quarters.

washers. Then stand the cabinet and, using spacer blocks ripped from scraps, position and hold the drawer dividers in place while you screw them to the sides. Keeping the dividers tight to the spacers as you screw them into place is important for the drawers to work properly.

IRON-ON EDGE BANDING

Edge-banding basics

If you've never used iron-on edge banding, it'll only take you a couple of attempts to achieve proficiency. Don't worry if you make a mistake; run the iron over it and the heat-sensitive glue will release so you can adjust the piece. Cut each strip of banding about 1 in. extra long with sharp scissors.

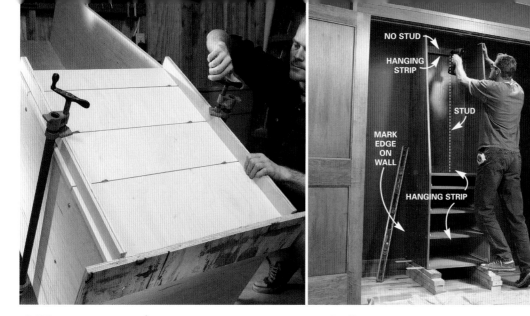

15 Lay a board across each edge of the fronts and clamp overnight. Then drive four 1-in. screws through each box into the fronts.

16 Set cabinet on blocks and center it in closet. Plumb it, shimming as needed, and drill 1/8-in. pilot holes through the cleats into studs or drywall.

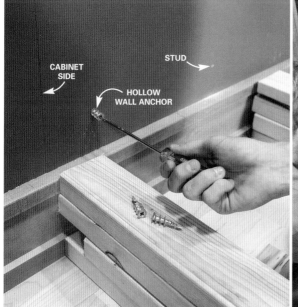

17 Remove the cabinet and screw drywall anchors into the holes without stud backing. Reposition the cabinet and screw it to the wall.

18 Build the shoebox about 1/2 in. short of the wall. Screw a cleat to the wall, then screw the box to the cabinet and nail it to the cleat.

Leave 1/2 in. or more of banding overhanging the starting corner because it tends to creep when you iron it. Move the iron (set on "cotton") along at about 1 in. per second all the way to the other end, guiding it with your other hand as you go. As you guide it, make sure the banding edges hang over each side of the plywood. Before it cools, push a block or roller over it to embed the banding. Then let the edge banding cool for

Handy Hints®

You'll save a lot of time simply by edge-banding all the parts after ripping them to width and before cutting them to length. Then you won't have so many individual parts to edge-band, or those pesky short drawer front ends to deal with. Pay attention to the simple little clamping tip using a shelf bracket shown in Photo 2.

19 Screw the closet rod brackets to the cleats and the cabinet, then install the clothes rods. Cut the top shelves and fasten them to cleats (Figure A).

20 Add the drawer pulls and adjustable shelves, then fill it up. *Still* not enough space? Donate whatever doesn't fit to charity!

30 seconds or so and check for voids. Re-iron and embed any loose spots.

Cut the ends as close to the plywood as possible with the scissors and then run the edge-band trimmer down both sides to trim off the overhang. You'll have to make multiple passes to get all of the spots flush. The trimmer works best if you trim with the grain. Sometimes that means reversing direction in the middle of trimming. Use a file held at a 45-degree angle to remove oozed-out glue and banding that's still a little proud, then sand all the joints smooth with a sanding block and 100-grit paper.

Drawer construction

Building drawers isn't all that hard. The key is to build the cabinet and the drawer boxes square. If you're using drawer slides other than the ones called for, read the directions before building the drawers. They'll tell you the necessary height and side-to-side clearances.

Building a square drawer is easy if you pin together the sides and then square them up with the plywood bottom (Photo 9). Accurate side-to-side dimensions are crucial (Figure B, p. 81). You can shim out the drawer slides if the drawers are narrow, but if they're too wide, rebuild them.

Now is a good time to finish ripping and edge-banding your adjustable and fixed shelves. Don't cut them to final width until the cabinet is mounted so you can measure and cut exact widths to fit their selected positions. Stain and finish everything at the same time prior to installation. An oil-based honey maple stain, and a top-coat of two coats of satin polyurethane was used here.

Making it fit in your closet

The cabinet unit is 78 in. tall, so it will fit in any closet with 8-ft. walls, even with the 6-in. gap at the floor. Alter the height if you have a lower ceiling.

You'll have to set the cabinet aside before mounting it to install drywall anchors unless you're lucky enough to have the cabinet fall in front of two studs. Position the cabinet in the closet, then plumb and mark the wall (Photo 17) so the pilot holes line up with the anchors after you reset it. Then measure to the wall to determine the final length for the top shelf—don't forget to add 1 in. for the left-side overhang. Place the cleats and shelves anywhere you wish.

making it fit your space

Build the cabinet taller, wider or with more drawers. Drawer sizes can be easily altered too—make deeper ones for sweaters or shallower ones for socks. The how-to steps shown here will work for any configuration that best suits your needs.

Gallery of ideas

The days of the "single-shelf, single-clothes rod closet" are gone. Organizing products ranging from hardworking laminate and wire systems to attractive furniture-quality units make better use of precious closet space. See Resources, p. 186, for more information.

Photo courtesy of Plato

Photo courtesy of ClosetMaid

Kidding around
Easily adjusted wire systems allow you to rearrange closet space as your kids grow and their needs change. The hanging clothes area can be converted from three tiers to two, or even one. Glide-out bins provide storage for toys and clothes alike.

The ultimate closet
This dream closet has a place for everything—and then some. Upper, lower and full-height cabinets provide concealed storage. Rolling ladders put even items in the overhead sections within reach.

section 4

free-standing and wall-mounted shelves

Traditional maple bookcase....90

Leaning tower of shelves 100

Entryway pocket screw
   coat locker 106

Coat and mitten rack 113

Swedish wall shelves..............116

Floating shelves–
   hollow door 120

Afternoon projects
   Portable bookshelf 124

   Easy-to-build
      display shelving...............124

   Closet rod and shelf............125

   Free-form wall shelves.......126

   Stud stuffer 127

   Petite shelves......................127

Traditional maple bookcase

Create your own classic bookcase with simple tools in these easy-to-follow steps

When you're ready to display your literary favorites, don't go to a furniture store and settle for a poorly constructed bookcase with zippo for detail. For about the cost of a cheap bookcase, you can build this handsome and solid heirloom-quality piece.

This project is too challenging for a beginner. Don't tackle it unless you've used a router and a doweling jig and feel confident with your circular saw. The project is broken into easy-to-follow steps and you have the option of selecting your own trim and finish.

The bookcase construction is straightforward and basic, so it's easy to cut and fit the pieces. The fixed shelves add stability and are designed to hold a variety of average-sized books, but you can customize the shelf heights to suit your collection.

The grooved vertical front pieces on each side (fluted casing) may look challenging, but with a shop-made jig and a router, you'll get perfect results. For details, see "Make your own fluted casing—the easy way," p. 96. Figure on about a day and a half for cutting and assembling, plus a couple of evenings for sanding and finishing.

project at a glance

skill level
intermediate to advanced

tools
router
doweling jig
miter saw
circular saw

cost
about $300–$400

Labels on left photo: TOP PIECE OF RIP GUIDE · RIP GUIDE · SAW BASE · LOWER EDGE OF RIP GUIDE · FACTORY EDGE · ALIGN YOUR MARK WITH THIS EDGE · PIECE BEING CUT FROM SHEET

Labels on right photo: EDGE GUIDE · 23/32" GROOVES · A

1 Rip 3/4-in. hardwood plywood into 11-1/4-in.-wide pieces for the sides and the shelves. Cut these pieces to length to make the two sides and the six shelves. Also cut the 1/4-in. plywood back to width and length while you have the edge guide set up.

2 Mark and cut the 1/4-in. dadoes in the sides. Use a special 23/32-in.-wide straight-cut router bit for a tight fit for the thinner-than-3/4-in. plywood.

All you need are simple hand and power tools

The only power tools you'll need are a 7/8-hp router, a circular saw (Photo 1) with a fine-toothed plywood blade, a drill, a power miter saw and an orbital sander. (And you could substitute a hand miter saw for the power one.) You'll also need other woodworking tools like C-clamps, bar clamps, spring clamps, a screwdriver, drill bits and a doweling jig (Photo 5) with a 3/8-in. brad point bit. Although you could get by without it, a 24-in. Clamp & Tool edge guide (Photo 2) is great for routing perfectly straight grooves (dadoes) to support the shelves (see Resources, p. 186). This tool clamps firmly to the edges of the plywood and leaves an unobstructed path to push your router from one side to the next. It's not a tool you'll get and use only once. The Clamp & Tool guide has dozens of uses, such as helping

making it fit your style

Our bookcase is made primarily from maple plywood and detailed with solid maple boards and regular lumberyard maple colonial stop molding (Figure A). If maple isn't your favorite wood, you could opt for birch and oak plywood and moldings. They, too, are commonly stocked in full-service lumberyards and good home centers.

you make super-straight crosscuts (perpendicular cuts to the wood grain) on lumber and plywood.

Get straight rip cuts with a homemade jig

If you've got a fancy setup for achieving perfectly straight cuts (rips) from a sheet of plywood on a table saw or something else, all the better. If you don't, this simple jig (Photo 1) is what you need.

Construct the jig by screwing together two scraps of either 1/2- or 3/4-in. plywood. The top narrow piece (2-1/2 in. wide) must have one factory straightedge. Leave the bottom piece a few inches wider than your saw base (in most cases, that will make the bottom piece about 10 in.). Screw the top piece to the bottom with drywall screws every 5 inches. Now you need to trim the lower piece perfectly straight.

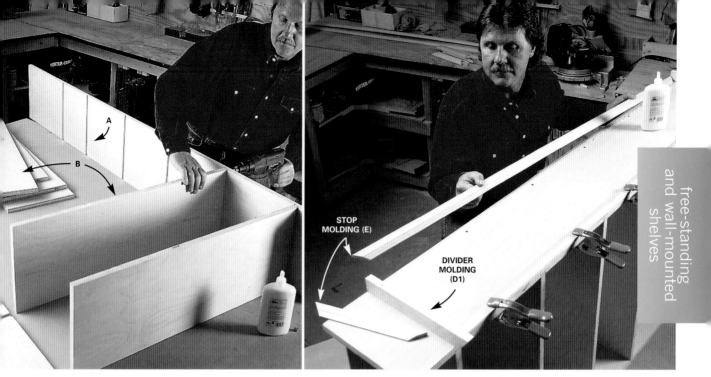

3 Glue and screw the shelves to the sides with 1-5/8-in. wood screws. Drill pilot and countersink holes no more than 3/4 in. from the front and back to accept the screws. The screws will be covered by molding later. Align the 1/4-in. plywood back (C) and square the assembly by nailing into the back of the sides and shelves.

4 Apply the divider and stop molding to the sides. Glue, then nail the divider molding to the sides with 6d finish nails (two per piece). Glue the stop molding to the sides as shown in Figure A. Further secure the molding with 7/8-in. brads spaced every 12 inches. Set the brads with a nail set. You'll fill the holes later with wood putty.

Now, clamp the jig to the entire piece of 3/4-in. maple plywood, setting it to the correct width. Rip-cut (lengthwise) the two bookcase sides (A), then cut them to length (crosscut). Rip two additional lengths and crosscut them (outer sides "A" facing up) into 31-7/8-in. lengths for the shelves. Cut the 1/4-in. plywood back (C) to the dimensions in the Cutting List, p. 94.

Rout the 1/4-in.-deep shelf slots into the sides

The shelves (B) lock into 1/4-in.-deep slots (dadoes) in the upright sides (A). To make the dadoes, install a 23/32-in. straight-cut router bit in your router and set the depth of cut to 1/4 inch. The special 23/32-in. router bit is the same width as 3/4-in. plywood, so the slots it cuts will make a nice snug fit for the shelves. Don't substitute a 3/4-in. bit; you'll be unhappy with the sloppy fit.

Clamp your edge guide (Photo 2) to a scrap piece of plywood and rout a test dado. Then measure the distance from the edge guide to the near edge of the dado. This will give you the distance you'll need for setting up each dado

groove. Mark and cut (see Figure A, p. 95) all the 1/4-in.-deep dadoes on the inside face of each part A. **TIP:** When you cut dadoes with a router and straightedge, clamp the edge guide to the left of your intended groove, then push the router base away from you as you rout the groove. This keeps the router tight against the edge guide as the bit rotates through the cut. Finish-sand all the plywood pieces now with 150-grit sandpaper; otherwise, you'll struggle with sanding in tight spaces after assembly.

Glue and screw the shelf ends into the slotted sides

It's essential to have a flat surface for assembly so you can align the shelves squarely to the sides. The shelves (B) should fit tightly into the grooves. Test the fit. If the shelf won't slip into the dado, wrap some fine sandpaper (150-grit) around a 1/2-in.-square block about 3 in. long and sand the sides of the grooves until you get a snug fit.

Once you're sure everything fits, you'll have to work fast to complete the assembly. You'll need to get the shelves glued into the dadoes and the 1/4-in. plywood back nailed into place before the glue sets (about 15 minutes). This means you need to get your drill, countersink bit and a power screwdriver and screws ready to go.

personally speaking

Spread a light coat of glue on one shelf side and into the dado, then fit each shelf into its dado. Have a moist cotton rag handy to wipe away any oozing glue. Next, screw the shelf to the side as shown in Figure A. The screw holes for each shelf side must be predrilled within 3/4 in. of the front and the back. The screwheads will be covered later by the molding. Follow this procedure for each shelf.

Now, before the glue sets, grab the 1/4-in. plywood back (C) to square the assembly. There's no need to glue the plywood back to the shelves or sides. First nail the back along one entire side using a 1-in. panel nail every 5 inches. Then align the top of the other side flush with the top edge of the plywood; this will square the assembly. Nail along this side, then nail the rest of the back into the backside of the shelves. Let the glue dry for at least two hours before continuing.

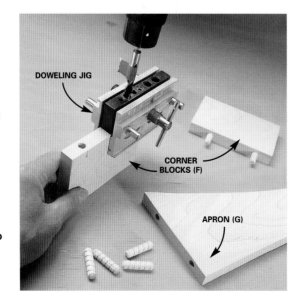

5 Drill 3/8-in. dowel holes in the corner blocks and corresponding holes in the aprons. Glue and clamp this assembly after you glue the stop moldings to the front of the blocks.

DOWELING JIG

CORNER BLOCKS (F)

APRON (G)

cutting list

KEY	PCS.	SIZE & DESCRIPTION
A	2	3/4" x 11-1/4" x 78" maple plywood sides
B	6	3/4" x 11-1/4" x 31-7/8" maple plywood shelves
C	1	1/4" x 32-3/4" x 76" maple plywood back
D1	6	3/4" x 1-1/2" x 13" maple divider molding*
D2	2	3/4" x 1-1/2" x 35-7/8" maple divider molding*
D3	2	3/4" x 1-1/2" x 4-5/8" maple divider caps*
E	80 ln. ft.	7/16" x 1-1/4" colonial stop molding (allows for waste)
F	4	3/4" x 3-1/2" x 5-1/2" maple corner blocks
G	2	3/4" x 5-1/2" x 26-3/4" maple curved aprons
H	2	3/4" x 3-1/2" x 64-3/4" maple fluted casing
J1	1	3/4" x 12-15/16" x 35-3/4" maple plywood top
J2	5-1/2 ln. ft.	3/4" x 3/4" maple edge banding*
K1	2	3/4" x 1-1/2" x 4" maple front feet*
K2	2	3/4" x 1-1/2" x 2" maple back feet*
L	2	3/4" x 5-1/2" x 11-1/4" support strips

*Have the lumberyard cut these pieces to width from a 1x6.

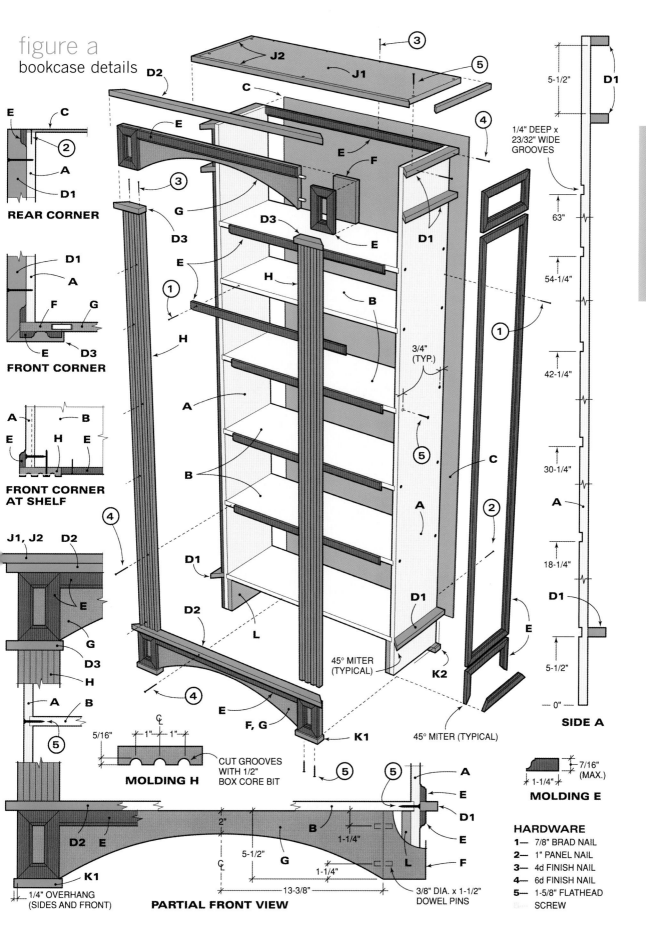

figure a
bookcase details

REAR CORNER
E · C · 2 · A · D1

FRONT CORNER
D1 · A · F · G · E · D3

**FRONT CORNER
AT SHELF**
A · B · E · H · E

J1, J2 · D2
E · G · D3 · H · A · B · 5

MOLDING H
5/16" · 1" · 1"
CUT GROOVES
WITH 1/2"
BOX CORE BIT

PARTIAL FRONT VIEW
D2 · E · K1
1/4" OVERHANG
(SIDES AND FRONT)
2" · 5-1/2" · 13-3/8"
G · B · 1-1/4" · 1-1/4" · A · E · D1 · E · L · F
3/8" DIA. x 1-1/2"
DOWEL PINS

J2 · J1 · C · E · E · F · E · D2 · 3 · 5 · 4
E · 3 · G · D3 · E · D3 · E · D1 · H · B · A · B · D1 · D2 · L · F, G · K1 · K2
45° MITER (TYPICAL) · 45° MITER (TYPICAL) · 3/4" (TYP.) · 1 · 2 · 5 · 4
F, G · E · 4

SIDE A
5-1/2" · D1
1/4" DEEP x
23/32" WIDE
GROOVES
63" · 54-1/4" · 42-1/4" · 30-1/4" · 18-1/4" · 5-1/2" · 0"
A · D1 · E · 1 · 2

MOLDING E
7/16" (MAX.) · 1-1/4"

HARDWARE
1— 7/8" BRAD NAIL
2— 1" PANEL NAIL
3— 4d FINISH NAIL
4— 6d FINISH NAIL
5— 1-5/8" FLATHEAD
SCREW

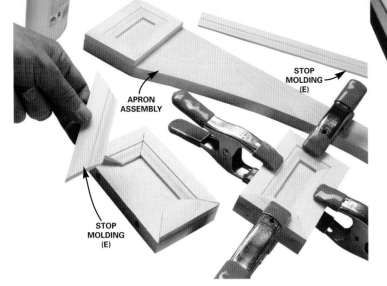

APRON
ASSEMBLY

STOP
MOLDING
(E)

STOP
MOLDING
(E)

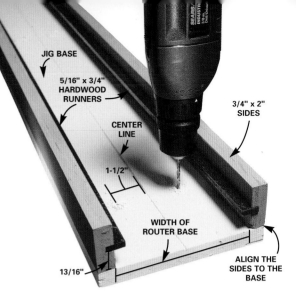

JIG BASE

5/16" x 3/4"
HARDWOOD
RUNNERS

CENTER
LINE

1-1/2"

3/4" x 2"
SIDES

WIDTH OF
ROUTER BASE

ALIGN THE
SIDES TO THE
BASE

13/16"

6 Glue the stop molding to the front of the corner blocks. Be very precise about the miter cuts. A simple wooden handsaw miter box works great for these small, hard-to-hold pieces. After the glue is set, sand the edges of the block with 100-grit, then 150-grit, sandpaper. Glue the dowel joints and clamp the corner blocks to the apron to complete the apron assemblies.

7 Drill holes 1-1/2 in. on both sides of the center line of your jig. Keep the holes about 4 in. back from each end and spaced about 2 ft. apart toward the middle. The holes are spaced 1-1/2 in. from the center to avoid having screw holes show through your flutes. If you rout a different width or number of flutes, you may need to change the hold-down screw locations. After drilling the holes, flip the jig over and countersink them to accept screws for holding the workpiece.

Detail the sides of the box with molding

Now it's time to detail the sides with the divider moldings (D1 and the lower D2; Figure A) and the colonial stop moldings. The divider molding, with the stop molding (Photo 4), breaks the strong vertical line to give the bookcase a distinct architectural look. It has a base section, a main vertical section and a top section similar to the cornice of a building.

To begin detailing the sides, first cut the divider molding, then glue and nail it (use 6d finish nails) to the sides (Photo 4). Drill pilot holes through the molding to prevent splitting. The colonial stop molding (E) and the backside of the divider molding must be applied so they align flush with the 1/4-in. plywood back. Glue and clamp this molding to the side. Drive 7/8-in. wire brads through the stop molding into the sides every 12 in., then set them.

Cut the corner blocks and apron

The decorative upper and lower corner blocks (Photo 6) are simple to make from 3/4-in.-wide x 5-1/2-in.-long pieces of solid maple. The detail on the front of the corner blocks is made by gluing mitered colonial stop molding to each block face. First cut the four corner blocks (F) and the

two curved aprons (G). Use a 27-1/2-in. radius to mark the curve onto the aprons. A nail, a wire and a pencil will work fine. Drill the dowel holes into the inside edge of the blocks and corresponding holes into the end of each apron. Don't glue these parts together yet. Mark the backside of each block and apron so you know which piece goes where.

Now to detail the corner blocks, miter the stop molding to fit the perimeter of each block. You can use a wooden handsaw miter box for control. Avoid cutting small pieces with the power miter saw. Once you've cut all the pieces, glue them to the blocks and clamp them with spring clamps (Photo 6). When the glue is dry, sand the edges of each block clean and glue the doweled joints for each upper and lower apron assembly. Clamp each assembly for at least two hours.

Make your own fluted casing— the easy way

There are a variety of ways to make decorative flutes for cabinet trim.

You can attach an edge guide to a router and run them down the length of the board three times. But if the router wanders even once, the piece is ruined.

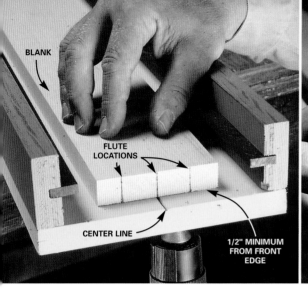

BLANK

FLUTE LOCATIONS

CENTER LINE

1/2" MINIMUM FROM FRONT EDGE

5/32" DEEP CUT

8 Mark your flute locations 1 in. apart on each end of your 1x4 blank. Align the center mark of the workpiece with the center line of the jig and screw the blank to the jig from underneath. Do the same on the opposite end and be sure to install the hold-down screws toward the middle as well. If your blank has a slight bow or crook, the hold-down screws will hold it straight and flat as you rout.

9 Rout the first pass of the first flute 5/32 in. deep. Don't try to take the whole depth at once, because you may get some tear-out and chatter. For a smooth cut, keep the router moving all the way to the other end in one continuous pass.

You can run the board through a router table, but there's a risk of creating burn marks while pausing to reposition your hands.

The jig shown here will help you churn out perfectly fluted pieces.

Build the fluting jig

Use one-third of a sheet (lengthwise) of 3/4-in. cabinet-grade plywood for the base and sides of the jig and two strips of hardwood for the runners (Photo 1). Here's how to measure, cut and assemble the jig:

- Measure the base of your router plus two thicknesses of your plywood sides (usually 23/32 in. each, or 1-7/16 in. total) to get the right width for the jig base.

- Rip the measured jig base width lengthwise (8 ft.) from your plywood sheet. Accuracy is critical; use your cutting guide for your circular saw or a table saw.

- Rip the two plywood sides 2 in. wide.

- Rip two runners 5/16 in. wide from a 3/4-in.-thick hardwood board.

- Cut the 5/16-in.-wide dadoes into the two sides using either a dado blade or multiple passes with a standard table saw blade. The dadoes must be 3/8 in. deep.

5/16" DEEP CUT

10 Rout a second pass with the router bit set at 5/16-in. depth. Be sure to check your router depth gauge so you can repeat the exact depth for the final pass on the next flutes.

- Glue (carpenter's glue works best) and screw the jig sides to the jig base (Photo 7). The sides must be flush with the base on each side. Drill pilot and countersink holes for the screws. Use a 1-1/4-in. screw every 8 in. along each side.

- Secure the hardwood runners into the dadoes using carpenter's glue and spring clamps. Set the jig aside to dry.

Once the jig is assembled, test the fit of your router base. Move it along the chute from end to end. It must

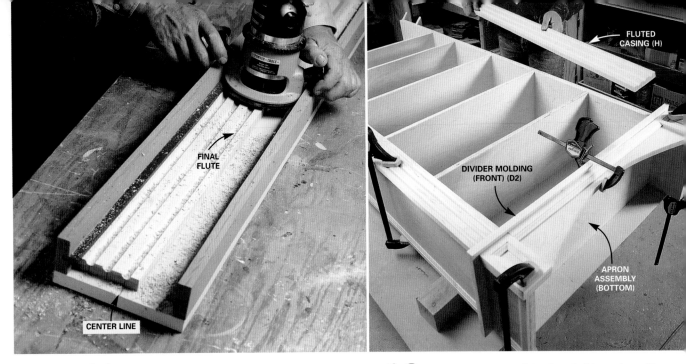

FLUTED CASING (H)

FINAL FLUTE

CENTER LINE

DIVIDER MOLDING (FRONT) (D2)

APRON ASSEMBLY (BOTTOM)

11 Rout each side flute using the same two-pass method as with the center flute. When the blank is positioned to the side of the jig, only one row of hold-down screws is necessary.

12 Align the bottoms of the fluted side casing with the corner blocks. Glue, clamp and nail the casing to the bookcase sides. Use six 6d finish nails per side. Set the nails and fill the nail holes.

safety smarts

Although stable on hard flooring, tall narrow cabinets like this bookcase can be unsteady when set on wall-to-wall carpeting. The 1/4-in.-thick tackless wood strip below the carpeting and near the wall can slightly elevate the back of the cabinet and make the bookcase tippy. You can remedy this problem by reducing the thickness of the back feet by 1/4 in. and attaching an 18-gauge steel safety wire, as shown below, near the center back of the cabinet. Fasten the other end of the wire to a stud.

Mark your bookcase height on the wall. Screw in a 2-1/2-in. drywall screw with a finish washer halfway into the wall stud, wrap the wire around the screw, then tighten the screw to the drywall.

Drive a 1-in. screw and finish washer near the back of the bookcase into the plywood top. Position the bookcase and wind the wire tight around the screw. Tighten the screw and finish wire down and cut the excess wire. Now you can pile on the books.

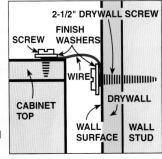

2-1/2" DRYWALL SCREW

FINISH WASHERS

SCREW

WIRE

DRYWALL

CABINET TOP

WALL SURFACE

WALL STUD

glide freely along the runners without binding on the sides. You may have to sand the sides a bit if the router is too tight in the chute. Conversely, if there's play between the router and the sides, install a strip of veneer on one side.

Now that you've made the jig, follow the instructions in Photos 7 – 11 and practice on some scrap pieces. To ensure consistent depth (you'll make two progressively deeper passes for each flute), familiarize yourself with the depth gauge on your router. It's usually a dial or ring on the housing.

Glue and nail your detail moldings to the bookcase front

Turn the bookcase on its back to glue the front trim pieces in place. Start by aligning the bottom edge of the lower apron assembly even with the bottom edge of the sides (A). Let the apron overhang the sides an equal amount. Mark this location. Next, glue and clamp the assembly (Photo 12) in place. Then, cut and glue the fluted casing pieces in place. Be sure they overhang the same distance as the lower apron assembly. For added insurance, nail the casing to the plywood sides with six 6d finish nails (Figure A) spaced evenly along the length.

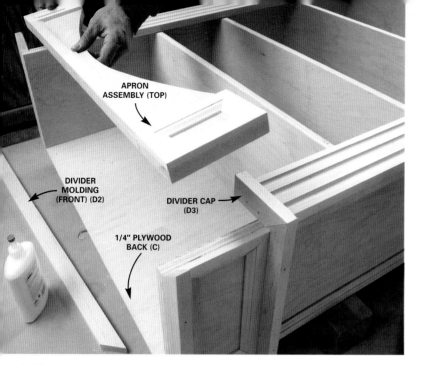

APRON ASSEMBLY (TOP)

DIVIDER MOLDING (FRONT) (D2)

DIVIDER CAP (D3)

1/4" PLYWOOD BACK (C)

13 **Glue the upper apron assembly to the sides after nailing the divider cap molding to the top of the casing. Once the apron assembly is glued, the next step is to glue, nail and clamp the top center section of the divider molding in place.**

Now glue and nail (Photo 13) the divider caps (D3) to the top of the fluted casing and to the side pieces of the divider molding (D1) with 4d finish nails. The caps are a continuation of the divider molding and establish an end point for the fluted columns. After the upper apron assembly is glued in place, glue the upper full-length divider molding (Figure A) to the top of the apron assembly and then nail the miter joints together with 4d nails.

Cut the plywood top and glue solid maple strips to the edge

Now cut and glue the stop molding (E) to the top of the plywood back. Use spring clamps to hold it in place. While the glue is drying, cut the plywood top (J1) and the 3/4 x 3/4-in. edge banding (J2) to length. Glue the molding around the front and sides of the plywood top. Use masking tape to hold the edging in place until the glue dries. Once the glue has dried, sand the edging flush to the plywood on the top and bottom. Screw the top assembly to the sides (A). Use 4d finish nails to secure the top to the stop molding in the back. Now cut the stop molding strips to cover the cut-edge shelf fronts. Secure the molding with glue and 7/8-in. brads. Set the brads and fill the holes with wood putty.

Screw the feet to the bottom

To complete the assembly, cut the front and back feet and secure each with two 1-5/8-in. wood screws. Be sure the support strips (L) are glued to the underside (Figure A) first to help support the feet. Cut the front and back feet and screw them to the bottom with 1-5/8-in. wood screws.

Wipe on a beautiful Danish oil finish

Bookcase projects like this are really tough to finish with a brush-on varnish after assembly, so use a wipe-on oil/varnish commonly called Danish oil. You can select colored oil/varnish or clear. The combination oil/varnish is as easy to apply as an oil and buffs to a nice luster like a brushed-on varnish. Apply the finish according to the manufacturer's instructions, using a cotton rag and keeping a brush on hand to get into the corners. Fill all the nail holes after the first coat of finish is dry. Use colored putty sticks to match the surrounding wood tone. Two coats of finish will be adequate but a third will give you a bit more luster and depth. *NOTE:* Hang the oil-soaked rags outside to dry to prevent combustion.

Leaning tower of shelves

This stylish but sturdy shelf unit will neatly hold your stuff—and you can build it in a day

This shelf unit may look lightweight and easy to topple. But don't be fooled. It's a real workhorse. The 33-1/2-in. x 82-3/4-in. tower features five unique, tray-like shelves of different depths to hold a wide variety of items up to 13-1/4 in. tall. Despite its 10-degree lean, the unit is surprisingly sturdy, and its open design won't overpower a room.

Whether you choose to make this piece more functional, as in this office setting, or place it in a family room to showcase treasures, the basic construction is the same. You select the type of wood and stain or paint to dress it up or down to fit the look of any room.

All the materials can be purchased at home centers or lumberyards. The only special tools you'll need are a power miter box for crisp angle cuts and an air-powered brad nailer for quick assembly and almost invisible joints. And you'll have to rustle up an old clothes iron for applying oak edge-banding material. Once you've gathered all the material, you can build the shelf unit in one afternoon.

Buying the wood

One note when buying boards: Use a tape measure to check the "standard" dimensions of 1x3s and 1x4s. They sometimes vary in width and thickness. Also check the two full-length 1x4s you plan to use as the uprights to be sure they're straight, without warps or twists. And always examine the ends, edges and surface for blemishes or rough areas that won't easily sand out.

Cut plywood shelves first

Lay a couple of 2x4s across sawhorses (Photo 1) to cut the half sheet of 3/4-in. plywood cleanly and without pinching the saw blade. Since all five shelves are 30-1/2 in. wide, cut this width first, making sure the grain will run the long way across the shelves. Remember to wear safety glasses, earplugs and a dust mask. Make a homemade jig to fit your circular saw and clamp it to the plywood (see Photos 1 and 2, p. 102).

Next, cut all five shelf depths, starting with the smallest shelf (3-3/8 in.) first. Cut smallest to largest so you'll have enough wood to clamp the jig. Make sure you account for the width of your saw blade when you cut each shelf.

Now mark and cut the top of all four 1x4 uprights (the end that rests against the wall), according to Photo 3 and the two dimensions provided in Figure B, p. 103. Use a sharp blade in your circular saw to prevent splintering. Then stow the sawhorses and move to the workbench.

Select the best front of each plywood shelf, clamp it to the bench on edge and sand it smooth with 150-grit paper on a sanding block. Then preheat a clothes iron to the "cotton" setting and run it over the top of the edge-banding veneer, making sure the veneer extends beyond all edges (Photo 4). Roll it smooth immediately after

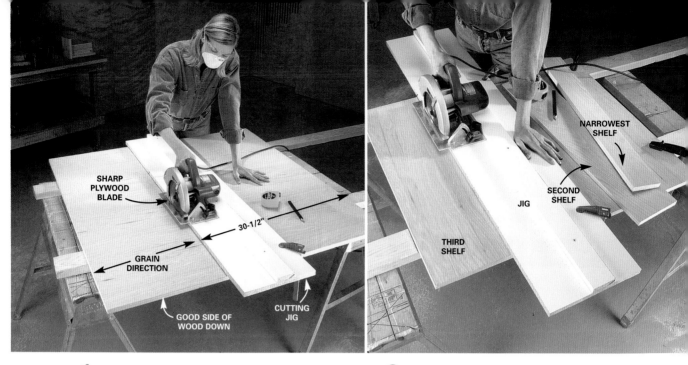

1 Cut 3/4-in. shelf plywood to width first, using a circular saw and a homemade jig for exact cuts. Use a sharp plywood blade and cut with the best side of the wood facing down to minimize splintering.

2 Cut the individual shelves, beginning with the narrowest, using the jig for perfectly straight cuts.

heating. Let each shelf edge cool for a couple of minutes before trimming and sanding the edges.

Cut the uprights and shelf frame next

Now enter the miter saw, which you use to make all the 90-degree straight cuts first (five shelf backs and 10 shelf sides; see Cutting List, p. 103). Remember that one end of each shelf side has a 10-degree cut, so we recommend first cutting them square at their exact length, then cutting the angle carefully so the long edge of each piece remains the same.

Next, rotate the miter saw table to the 10-degree mark and cut all the angle pieces. First cut the bottom of both uprights so each upright rests flat against the floor and wall (see Figure A, p. 103). Then trim the top of the upright to match the bottom, being careful to maintain the 84-in. total length. Next, cut the cleats based on the Cutting List dimensions, which are measured edge to edge (Photo 5 and Figure A). Leave the top cleats long and cut them to exact fit during assembly. Then, to speed finishing, use an orbital sander with 150-grit sand-paper to smooth all pieces before assembly.

Assemble uprights first, then the shelves

To begin assembly, lay out both uprights and all cleats to ensure that the angles are correct so the shelves will be level when the unit is against the wall. Then glue and nail the first cleat flush with the base of each upright (using five or six 1-1/4-in. brads) on each cleat. Work your way upward using 1x3 spacers (Photo 6). Make sure the spacer is the exact same width as the shelf sides! Set these aside to dry.

For shelf assembly, first glue and nail on the shelf backs. Next, apply the sides with glue and nails (Photo 7).

For final assembly, lay one upright on 2x4s, then clamp on

shopping list

- One half sheet (4' x 4') of 3/4" oak plywood
- Three 8' oak 1x3s
- Four 8' oak 1x4s
- One package (25') of 7/8" oak iron-on veneer (Band-It brand, The Cloverdale Co., www.band-itproducts.com, 800-782-9731, purchased at Home Depot)
- Veneer edge trimmer (Band-It brand; see above and click "Retail," "Related Products")
- Wood glue
- 1-1/4" brad nails
- Foam pads (1 pkg. of 3/4" round, self-adhesive non-skid pads)

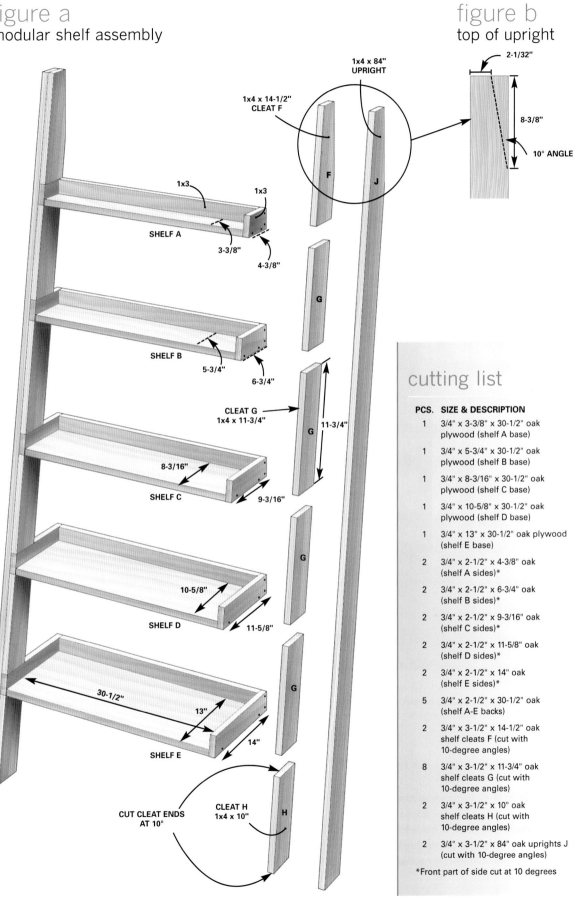

figure a
modular shelf assembly

1x4 x 84"
UPRIGHT

1x4 x 14-1/2"
CLEAT F

1x3

1x3

SHELF A

3-3/8"

4-3/8"

SHELF B

5-3/4"

6-3/4"

CLEAT G
1x4 x 11-3/4"

G

11-3/4"

8-3/16"

SHELF C

9-3/16"

10-5/8"

SHELF D

11-5/8"

G

30-1/2"

13"

14"

SHELF E

CUT CLEAT ENDS
AT 10°

CLEAT H
1x4 x 10"

H

F

J

G

figure b
top of upright

2-1/32"

8-3/8"

10° ANGLE

cutting list

PCS.	SIZE & DESCRIPTION
1	3/4" x 3-3/8" x 30-1/2" oak plywood (shelf A base)
1	3/4" x 5-3/4" x 30-1/2" oak plywood (shelf B base)
1	3/4" x 8-3/16" x 30-1/2" oak plywood (shelf C base)
1	3/4" x 10-5/8" x 30-1/2" oak plywood (shelf D base)
1	3/4" x 13" x 30-1/2" oak plywood (shelf E base)
2	3/4" x 2-1/2" x 4-3/8" oak (shelf A sides)*
2	3/4" x 2-1/2" x 6-3/4" oak (shelf B sides)*
2	3/4" x 2-1/2" x 9-3/16" oak (shelf C sides)*
2	3/4" x 2-1/2" x 11-5/8" oak (shelf D sides)*
2	3/4" x 2-1/2" x 14" oak (shelf E sides)*
5	3/4" x 2-1/2" x 30-1/2" oak (shelf A-E backs)
2	3/4" x 3-1/2" x 14-1/2" oak shelf cleats F (cut with 10-degree angles)
8	3/4" x 3-1/2" x 11-3/4" oak shelf cleats G (cut with 10-degree angles)
2	3/4" x 3-1/2" x 10" oak shelf cleats H (cut with 10-degree angles)
2	3/4" x 3-1/2" x 84" oak uprights J (cut with 10-degree angles)

*Front part of side cut at 10 degrees

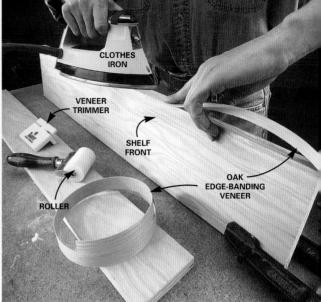

3 Cut both shelf uprights to length with a miter saw. Clamp to sawhorses. Mark the 10-degree angle at the top (dimensions in Figure B), then cut with a circular saw.

TOP OF UPRIGHT

10° ANGLE REMOVED

CLOTHES IRON

VENEER TRIMMER

SHELF FRONT

ROLLER

OAK EDGE-BANDING VENEER

4 Iron edge-banding veneer to the front edge of all five shelves. Roll the entire surface to ensure a solid bond, and trim the edges.

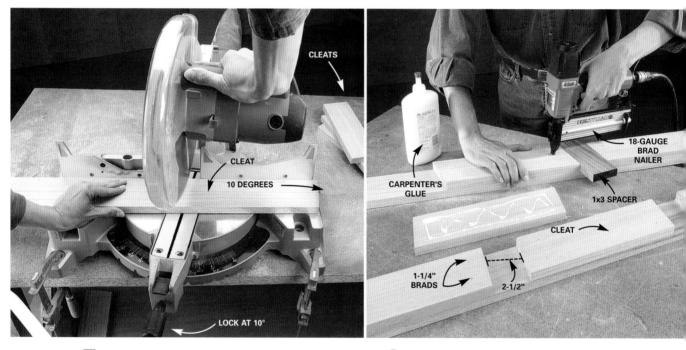

CLEATS

CLEAT

10 DEGREES

LOCK AT 10°

18-GAUGE BRAD NAILER

CARPENTER'S GLUE

1x3 SPACER

CLEAT

1-1/4" BRADS

2-1/2"

5 To maintain accuracy, lock the miter box at 10 degrees, then cut all angled pieces—uprights, cleats and one end of shelf sides—without changing the table.

6 Glue and nail the shelf cleats to the uprights using a 1x3 spacer. Hold each cleat tight to the spacer.

safety smarts

The shelf is highly stable as designed, but once you've stained or painted it, you can add self-adhesive foam gripping pads to the bottom of the uprights. And if you don't feel secure having it on a slippery floor, the unit's width is perfect for screwing the top of the uprights into wall studs.

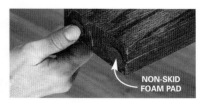

NON-SKID FOAM PAD

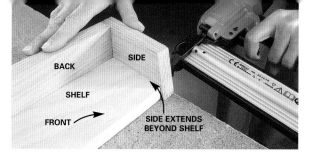

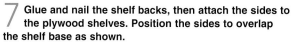

7 Glue and nail the shelf backs, then attach the sides to the plywood shelves. Position the sides to overlap the shelf base as shown.

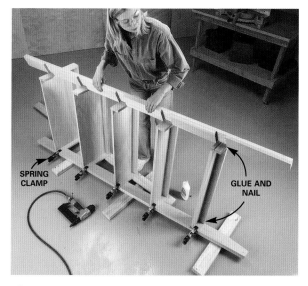

8 Clamp the shelves into one upright. Spread glue in the shelf notches of the other upright, position it flush with the front of the shelves and nail. Flip the unit over and attach the other upright.

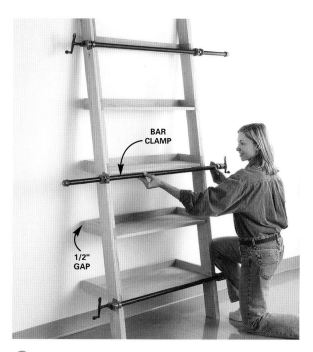

9 Set the shelf unit against a straight wall, check for squareness and apply three bar clamps until the glue dries.

the shelves as shown in Photo 8. Apply the glue, position the second upright on top flush with the front edge of the shelves, then sink four 1-1/4-in. brads into each shelf from the upright side. Carefully turn the unit over and repeat the process to attach the second upright. Work quickly so the glue doesn't set.

making it fit your style

This unit is built with red oak and oak veneer plywood, and finished with two coats of red oak stain. The beauty of this project is that any wood species will work. If you plan to paint it, select alder or aspen for the solid parts and birch for the plywood.

Lift the ladder shelf and place it upright against a straight wall. Check it with a framing square and flex it if necessary to square it up and to make sure that the uprights rest flat against the floor and wall (assuming your floor is level). Attach three bar clamps as shown in Photo 9 while the glue dries.

Handy Hints®

To minimize splintering when cutting plywood with a circular saw, always:
- Use a sharp plywood-cutting blade
- Set the blade depth so it cuts only 1/4 in. deeper than the plywood
- Cut "good side down" and make sure the plywood is supported well

Entryway pocket screw coat locker

Intimidated by cabinet work? Even a novice can make fine joints with pocket screws.

If you've ever seen a pocket screw jig being demonstrated at a woodworking show, you'll know how this simple tool will enable you to quickly and painlessly assemble tight-fitting joints without investing in a bunch of expensive clamps or special tools.

Pocket screw joints are best described as a screw version of toenailing, where boards are joined by angling a fastener through the edge of one into the other. The concept is simple, but the precisely engineered drill guide (the jig), drill bit and pocket screws are what make the system so easy and foolproof.

project at a glance

skill level
intermediate

tools
pocket screw jig kit
power miter box
drill
power sanders
circular saw
basic hand tools

cost
about $400–$450

Buy a good pocket screw jig

You can purchase a $65 kit that contains the Kreg "Rocket" jig shown on p. 110, the special clamp and the stepped drill bit with a stop collar and square driver bit. Avoid the temptation to buy an inexpensive jig; you'll never experience the real benefits of pocket screws if you're frustrated by a poorly designed tool. Less-expensive jigs lack the self-aligning lip and built-in clamp found on this and other high-quality models. You can get higher-priced pocket hole jigs that have more elaborate clamping systems and built-in motors to speed up the operation, but the end result is essentially the same.

The joinery system is incomplete without the specially designed pocket screws. These screws have a narrow shank with a thread-cutting tip to avoid splitting hardwoods, and a strong head with a square recess for slip-proof driving. The most common length is 1-1/4 in., the best size for joining 3/4-in.-thick material. Corrosion-resistant exterior screws, washer head screws for joining particleboard, and hi-lo thread screws for softwood are also available. To check out the various types, order an assortment for about $20 from the Kreg Tool Company (see Resources, p. 186).

Building the coat locker

The coat locker we built is constructed of 3/4-in. birch plywood with 3/4-in. solid-birch boards for the face frame, drawer sides and front, baseboard and top edge. The back and drawer bottoms are 1/4-in. birch plywood. The plywood and boards shown here were purchased from a local hardwood lumber supplier. This is usually the best source for good-quality hardwood boards, and you can have them cut to the right width and planed smooth on all four edges. You can also get your materials at home centers and full-service lumberyards.

Even though this coat locker is built with simple pocket screw joints, many of the parts must be cut to precise dimensions. You can use a circular saw guided by a clamped straightedge to cut the plywood. You'll need a power miter box ($25 a day to rent) for cutting the

face frame, edge band, drawer sides and moldings.

Cut out the plywood parts and drill pocket holes in the horizontal fixed shelves (A) and top and bottom pieces (also A). See Photo 1. For this project, the pocket holes will either be hidden from view or filled, so there's no need to precisely locate the holes.

Join all of the horizontal panels (A) to the sides and uprights (B1 and B2) with pocket screws, making sure to face the screw holes to the hidden or least conspicuous side (Photo 2). Check the cabinet box for square by measuring diagonally across the corners. Now you can use the box as a pattern for cutting out and joining the face-frame parts.

Cut the 3/4-in. solid-birch face frame parts to length using a power miter box. For tight-fitting joints, the edges of the boards must be square to the face and the end joints cut perfectly square. Bore the pocket screw holes (Photo 3). Now assemble the frame without glue and set it onto the box to check the fit. Take the frame apart, adjust the size if necessary, reassemble it using glue, and attach it to the box (Photos 4 and 5).

Photos 6 and 7 show how to assemble the drawer box and attach the slides. You can use the inexpensive epoxy-coated drawer slides, as shown, but for better access to the drawer interior, you could install full-extension slides instead. Use whatever shimming material you have around to build out the sides of the drawer compartments flush with the edge of the face frame. Then you can mount the slide as shown in Photo 7.

Attaching the drawer front (T) so it's perfectly aligned is a little tricky. Start by drilling four 5/16-in. holes in the front of the drawer box. Place the drawer in the opening.

shopping list

ITEM	QTY.
3/4" x 4' x 8' birch plywood	2
1/4" x 4' x 8' birch plywood	1
1x2 x 12' birch or maple board	2
1x3 x 6' birch or maple board	2
1x4 x 6' birch or maple board	2
1x6 x 8' birch or maple board	1
1x6 x 5' birch or maple board	1
1x8 x 3' birch or maple board	1
11/16" x 1-3/8" x 6' birch base cap	1
9/16" x 2" x 6' birch cove molding	1
2x4 x 3' scrap for fillers	
1-1/4" pocket screws	130
1-1/4" drywall screws	8
No. 8 x 1-1/4" pan head screws	8
No. 10 finish washers	8
6d finish nails	1 lb.
1" x 17-gauge brads	1 pkg.
1" paneling nails	1 pkg.
Carpenter's glue	8 oz.
Blum B230M 12" drawer slides	2 pair
Coat hooks	6
Drawer knobs	2
Benjamin Moore No. 241 Colonial Maple stain	1 qt.
Black stain	1 pt.
Sanding sealer	1 qt.
Satin finish varnish	1 qt.
Interior wood primer and paint	

cutting list

KEY	QTY.	SIZE & DESCRIPTION
PLYWOOD BOX		
A	8	3/4" x 13-3/4" x 16-7/8" horizontals
B1	2	3/4" x 14" x 72" sides
B2	1	3/4" x 13-3/4" x 72" upright
C	1	3/4" x 14-7/8" x 36-1/4" top
D	1	1/4" x 35-1/2" x 72" back
FACE FRAME PARTS		
E	1	3/4" x 5-1/2" x 31" bottom rail
F	1	3/4" x 3" x 31" top rail
G	4	3/4" x 1-1/2" x 14-3/4" intermediate rails
H	2	3/4" x 2-1/2" x 72" side rails
J	1	3/4" x 1-1/2" x 62-7/8" middle rail
TRIM AND EDGE BAND		
K1	2	3/4" x 1-1/2" x 17" edge band*
K2	1	3/4" x 1-1/2" x 40" edge band*
L1	2	3/4" x 3" x 16" base*
L2	1	3/4" x 3" x 40" base*
M1	2	11/16" x 1-3/8" x 16" base cap*
M2	1	11/16" x 1-3/8" x 40" base cap*
N1	2	9/16" x 2" x 17" cove molding*
N2	1	9/16" x 2" x 40" cove molding*
P	2	3/4" x 3-1/2" x 16-7/8" hook strips

*Miter-cut to finished lengths during assembly

KEY	QTY.	SIZE & DESCRIPTION
DRAWER PARTS		
Q	4	3/4" x 12-1/4" x 4-3/4" ends
R	4	3/4" x 13" x 4-3/4" sides
S	2	1/4" x 13-3/4" x 13" plywood bottom
T	2	3/4" x 5-13/16" x 14-9/16" fronts
U	4	1" x 2" x 6-3/4" fillers
V	2	3/4" x 6-3/4" x 13-3/4" filler panels
W	2	3/8" x 1-1/2" x 13-3/4" filler strips

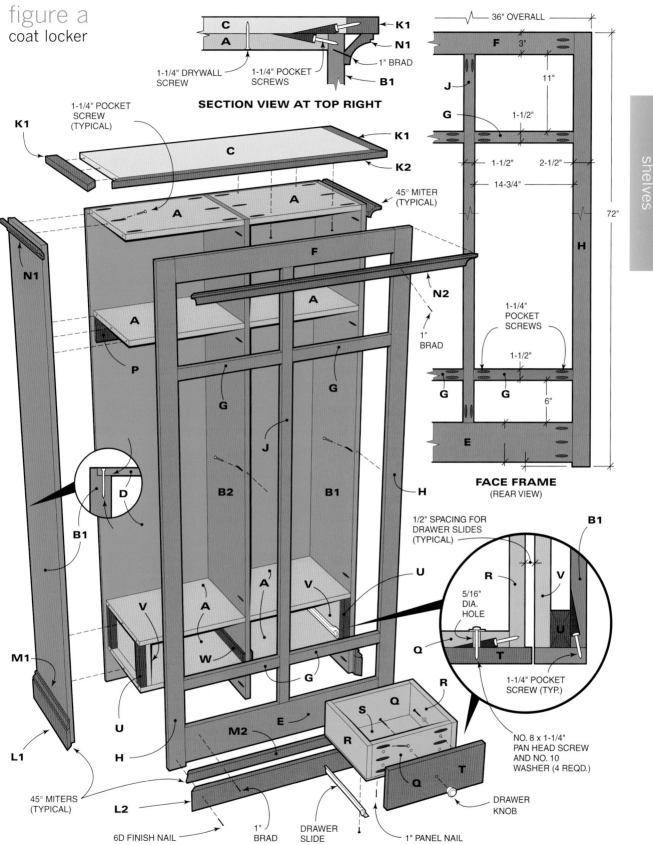

figure a
coat locker

SECTION VIEW AT TOP RIGHT

1-1/4" DRYWALL SCREW

1-1/4" POCKET SCREWS

1" BRAD

K1

N1

B1

C
A

36" OVERALL

3"

11"

1-1/2"

1-1/2"

2-1/2"

14-3/4"

72"

1-1/4" POCKET SCREWS

1-1/2"

6"

F
J
G
H
G
G
E

FACE FRAME
(REAR VIEW)

1-1/4" POCKET SCREW (TYPICAL)

K1

K1
K2

C

45° MITER (TYPICAL)

A
A

N2

1" BRAD

N1

A
P

F

A

G
J
G

D
B1

B2
B1

H

1/2" SPACING FOR DRAWER SLIDES (TYPICAL)

B1

5/16" DIA. HOLE

R
V
U

Q
T

1-1/4" POCKET SCREW (TYP.)

V
A
V
U
W
A
G

U
M1

E
M2

S
Q

R
R

Q
T

DRAWER KNOB

NO. 8 x 1-1/4" PAN HEAD SCREW AND NO. 10 WASHER (4 REQD.)

L1

45° MITERS (TYPICAL)

H

L2

6D FINISH NAIL

1" BRAD

DRAWER SLIDE

1" PANEL NAIL

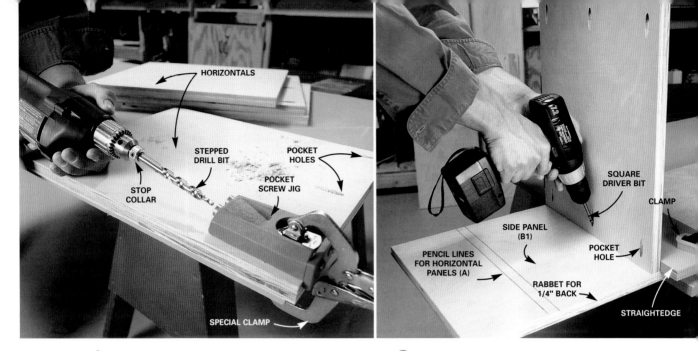

1 Clamp the pocket hole jig to the horizontal panel (A) and workbench. Follow the manufacturer's instructions for setting the stop collar on the special bit to the correct depth. Insert the bit into the jig's metal sleeve before you turn on the drill. Start the drill so the bit is turning at full speed (2,000 rpm is recommended). Then bore the clearance and pilot hole in one step by pushing the bit into the workpiece until the stop collar contacts the metal sleeve. Bore three holes on both ends of the eight horizontal panels.

2 Lay out the horizontal panel (A) locations with a framing square. Then clamp a straightedge along the line to hold the panels in position while you drive in the 1-1/4-in. pocket screws. Attach all eight panels (A) to the uprights (B1 and B2).

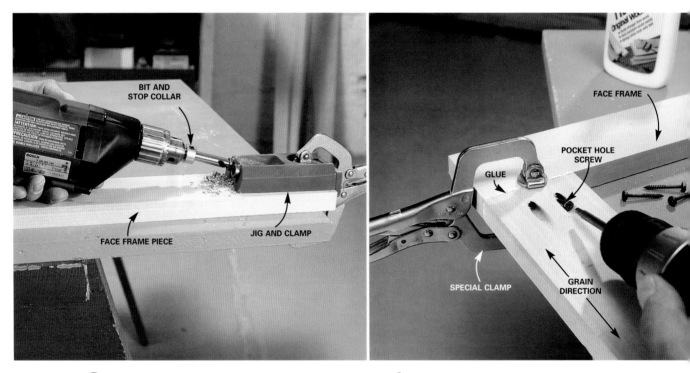

3 Clamp the jig to the end of a face frame board and bore holes for two pocket screws. Drill the opposite end, and all other face-frame parts that need pocket screw holes. Remember that only one half of each joint needs pocket screw holes. Drill parallel to the grain, as shown.

4 Spread wood glue on both pieces to be joined. Clamp the joint together to hold the faces flush, and drive in the 1-1/4-in. pocket screws. We used a special locking pliers–type clamp provided by the jig manufacturer.

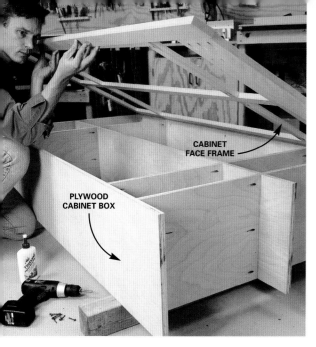

CABINET
FACE FRAME

PLYWOOD
CABINET BOX

5 Attach the face frame to the box. First bore pocket screw holes every 16 in. along the inside front edge of the box, placing them in concealed locations when possible. After checking the alignment, spread an even layer of wood glue on the edge of the plywood and use a clamp to hold the frame in position while you attach it to the box with pocket screws. Remove excess glue with a damp rag. When the glue is dry, sand the outside edge of the face frame flush with the box, being careful not to sand through the thin veneer on the plywood.

Use double-faced carpet tape or hot-melt glue to temporarily secure the drawer front to the drawer box. Gently open the drawer and clamp the front to the box. Attach it with four No. 8 x 1-1/4-in. pan head screws with No. 10 finish washers under the heads. Snug the screws but don't tighten them. The extra-large holes will allow you to tap the drawer front into exact alignment before you fully tighten the screws.

Construct the cabinet top by attaching edging strips (K1 and K2) to the plywood (C) with pocket screws (Photo 8). Use this same procedure for edge-gluing boards for a tabletop or attaching wood nosing to a counter.

Complete the cabinet as shown in Photo 9. Glue wood plugs, available from the Kreg Company (see Resources,

free-standing and wall-mounted shelves

pros and cons of pocket screws

Pocket screw joints have many advantages over more traditional joinery:

● **You can assemble large frames without needing an arsenal of expensive clamps** because the screws provide the clamping action while the glue dries.

● **No fancy cutting is required;** joints are simply butted together, saving time and reducing tool costs.

● **The use of an alignment clamp during assembly ensures flush joints** without any tricky measuring.

Pocket screw joints aren't perfect:

● **Every joint leaves behind a long, oblong hole** that looks bad when it's prominent, like on cabinet doors. Luckily, you can order wood plugs in just about any species to fill these odd holes—you just glue them in and sand them flush. Dowels, biscuits or mortise-and-tenon joints would be a better choice if the backside of a joint will be highly visible.

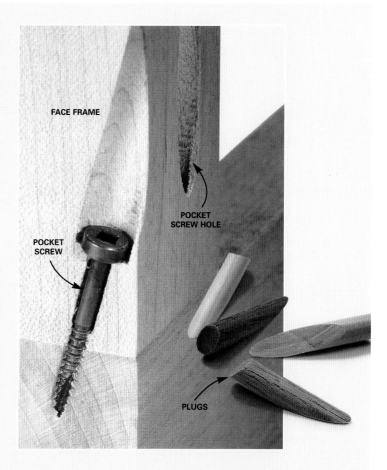

FACE FRAME

POCKET SCREW HOLE

POCKET SCREW

PLUGS

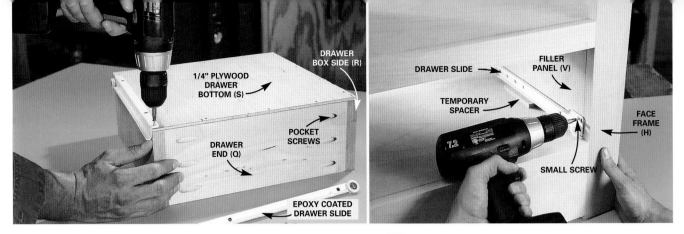

6 Cut 1x6 boards to form a box that is 13 in. long and exactly 1 in. narrower than the drawer opening in the face frame. Bore pocket holes on the end drawer pieces (Q) as shown and screw the box together. Use a framing square to square up the drawer. Then nail on the 1/4-in. plywood bottom with 1-in. paneling nails. Attach the 12-in. epoxy-coated slides to the drawer with the screws provided, aligning the front (the end without the wheel) of the slide with the front of the drawer box.

7 Shim the sides of the drawer compartments flush to the face frame with scraps of plywood and shims ripped to the proper thickness. Then attach the other half of the drawer slides, holding the front edge of the slide even with the front edge of the face frame. (Check the manufacturer's specifications for exact placement.) Use a spacer to hold the drawer slide parallel to the cabinet bottom while you screw it in.

8 Band the edge of the plywood top with 1-1/2-in. strips of birch (K1 and K2), mitered to fit. Spread wood glue on both edges and secure the 1x2 band to the plywood (C) with pocket screws as shown. Wipe off the excess glue with a damp rag. Use an orbital sander to sand the 1x2 flush with the plywood. Position the top on the cabinet so that an equal amount hangs over both sides and the front. Hold the top in place with a clamp while you attach it through the top of the cabinet box with 1-1/4-in. drywall screws.

9 Mark, miter and nail on the 2-in. cove (N1 and N2), the 3/4-in. x 3-in. base (L1, L2) and the 1-5/8-in. base cap (M1 and M2). Use 6d finish nails for the base, and 1-in. brads to attach the moldings. Drill pilot holes for the nails to avoid splitting the moldings. Attach the hook strips with pocket screws. Then cut a piece of 1/4-in. plywood (D) to fit the back and attach it with 1-in. paneling nails. Draw lines to indicate dividers to help in placing the nails accurately.

p. 186), into the exposed pocket holes on the cabinet interior and sand them flush.

Now you know how to use pocket screws in some of the more common cabinetmaking applications, but don't ignore other possibilities. Once you get the pocket screw joining bug, you can come up with your own innovative uses for this ingenious little connector.

Coat and mitten rack

Simple hand tools plus a few hours of work make for a handsome, functional gift

This simple coat rack is easy to build with butt joints connected by screws that are hidden with wooden screw-hole buttons and wood plugs. It mounts easily to the wall with screws driven through the hidden hanging strip on the back. The five large Shaker pegs are great for holding hats, umbrellas and coats and the hinged-hatch door at the top keeps the clutter of gloves and scarfs from view.

You can build this project in a few hours with an additional hour to apply a finish. Maple is an ideal wood for Shaker-style pieces, but any

project at a glance

skill level
beginner

tools
jig saw
drill
circular saw

cost
about $70

hardwood will do. Figure on spending about $70 for wood, hardware and varnish.

Cutting the pieces

First transfer the pattern measurements in Figure A, p. 114, using a compass, and then cut the sides (A) with a jig saw. Next cut the top (D) to length and rip the shelf (B) to the width given in the Cutting List. Cut the hanging strip (F) and the peg strip (C) to the same length as the shelf (B). Now drill the 3/8-in. counterbore holes for the screw-hole buttons (with your spade bit) 3/16 in. deep into the outsides of parts A (as

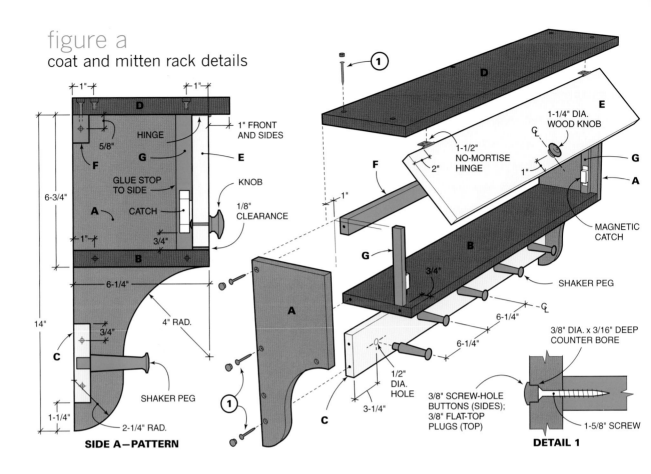

figure a
coat and mitten rack details

1" FRONT AND SIDES

HINGE

5/8"

G

F

E

GLUE STOP TO SIDE

KNOB

A

CATCH

1/8" CLEARANCE

6-3/4"

1"

3/4"

D

B

6-1/4"

4" RAD.

14"

3/4"

C

1-1/4"

SHAKER PEG

2-1/4" RAD.

SIDE A—PATTERN

1

A

C

G

1

3-1/4"

1/2" DIA. HOLE

D

E

1-1/4" DIA. WOOD KNOB

1-1/2" NO-MORTISE HINGE

2"

F

1"

G

A

B

G

3/4"

6-1/4"

6-1/4"

MAGNETIC CATCH

SHAKER PEG

3/8" DIA. x 3/16" DEEP COUNTER BORE

3/8" SCREW-HOLE BUTTONS (SIDES); 3/8" FLAT-TOP PLUGS (TOP)

1-5/8" SCREW

DETAIL 1

---

shown in Figure A, and Photo 2). Also drill the 3/8-in. counterbore holes in the top. These holes must be 3/8 in. deep.

Mark and drill the 1/2-in. holes for the Shaker pegs in the peg strip. Drill the holes for the Shaker pegs perfectly perpendicular to the peg strip to ensure they all project evenly when glued in place.

Assembly

Lay the pieces on your workbench, as shown in Photo 3. Align the hanging strip (F), the shelf (B), and the peg strip (C) as shown and clamp the sides (A) to these parts. Predrill the holes with a combination pilot hole/countersink bit using the center of the counterbore holes as a guide. Next, screw the sides to B, C and F. Fasten the top (D) to the sides in the same manner.

Handy Hints®

Sight down the edge of the peg strip to perfectly align each peg as the glue sets.

Glue and clamp the hatch stops to the insides of parts A, as shown in Figure A. To finish the assembly, cut the hatch (E) to size and install the hinges to the underside of part D and the top of the hatch. Now glue the buttons and pegs into their corresponding holes. Use only a small drop of glue for the buttons but be sure to apply a thin layer of glue completely around the plugs. This will swell the plugs for a tight fit. After the glue is dry, trim the two pegs flush with the top.

Finishing

Lightly sand the entire piece after assembly with 220-grit sandpaper. Apply two coats of clear Danish oil to all the surfaces (remove the hinges and knobs). Once the finish is dry, add two magnetic catches to the hatch-stop molding (G).

miscellaneous

ITEM	QUANTITY
1-1/2" no-mortise hinges*	1 pair
1-1/4" beech knob*	1
Narrow magnetic catch*	2
3-3/8" long Shaker pegs*	5
3/8" screw hole buttons*	10
3/8" plugs*	5
3/8" spade bit	1
1/2" spade bit	1
1-5/8" wood screws	15
Carpenter's glue	1 pint
Danish oil	1 pint
150- and 220-grit sandpaper	

* Available from home centers and woodworking specialty stores and Internet sites.

cutting list

KEY	PCS.	SIZE & DESCRIPTION
A	2	3/4" x 6-1/4" x 14" maple sides
B	1	3/4" x 6-1/4" x 32-1/2" maple shelf
C	1	3/4" x 3-1/2" x 32-1/2" maple peg strip
D	1	3/4" x 7-1/4" x 36" maple top
E	1	3/4" x 5-13/16" x 32-5/16" maple hatch
F	1	3/4" x 1-1/4" x 32-1/2" maple hanging strip
G	2	3/4" x 1/2" x 6" maple hatch stop

safety smarts

Be sure this project is screwed to the wall studs. Drill two holes into the hanging strip at stud locations and use 2-1/2-in. or longer wood screws.

1 Cut the side pieces (A) using a jig saw or band saw. Sand the curved edges smooth with a 1-1/2-in. drum sander.

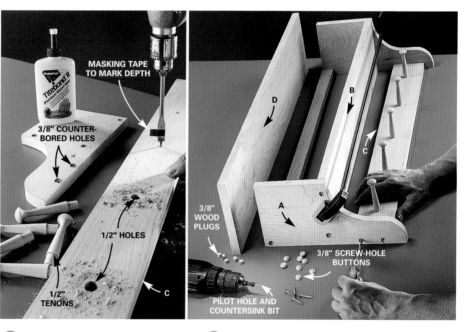

2 Drill the 1/2-in. holes 5/8 in. deep for the 3-3/8-in. Shaker pegs and the 3/8-in. counterbore holes 3/16 in. deep for the screw-hole buttons in parts A.

3 Assemble the shelf by clamping parts C, F and B to the sides. Drill pilot holes and screw the pieces together. The screws will be covered by the buttons and plugs.

Swedish wall shelves

Scandinavian charm in an afternoon

Here's a charming shelf that's small enough to fit on any wall and can be built in an afternoon. It makes a great gift and it's easy to make a bunch all at once. While the design is based on a 19th-century Swedish-American clock shelf, its use today is limited only by your imagination. Kitchen spice shelf, photo display shelf, knickknack shelf—it's great for just about anything, except maybe a set of encyclopedias!

Getting started

You'll need a scroll saw to cut out the parts for this project. In a pinch a bandsaw could do the job, but you'll have a lot more sanding to do on the edges. Because the parts for this shelf are small enough to fit around knots and defects, you can save some money by ordering a lower grade of wood called #1 or #2 common.

project at a glance

skill level
intermediate to advanced

tools
scroll saw
clamps
drill

cost
about $10–$15

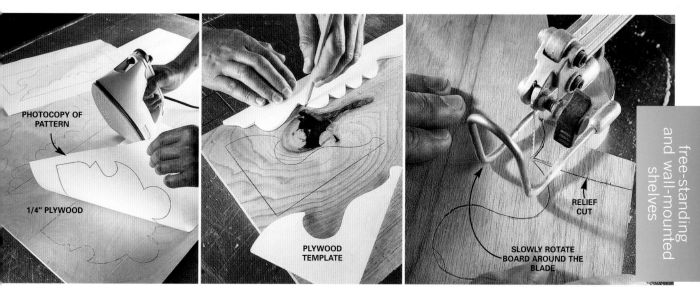

1 Iron on a photocopy of the patterns using a household iron set on high with no steam. If you're building several shelves, transfer the patterns onto a piece of 1/4-in. birch plywood to make reusable templates. Or, for a single shelf, spray some low-tack mounting adhesive on the back of each paper pattern and stick it right onto the wood.

PHOTOCOPY OF PATTERN

1/4" PLYWOOD

2 Trace the outline of your template onto the wood. Take advantage of grain patterns around knots that follow the shape of your piece.

PLYWOOD TEMPLATE

3 Cut out the pieces on the scroll saw. For tight inside corners like this use what's called a "zero-radius" turn. Here's how to do it: Cut all the way into the corner, then rotate the piece around the blade by letting the teeth slowly nibble away as you complete the turn. If you've never done a zero-radius turn before you can always make relief cuts into the corners to give your blade more room.

RELIEF CUT

SLOWLY ROTATE BOARD AROUND THE BLADE

For the shelf shown here, #1 common butternut was used. It cost about 1/3 less than select grade would have cost. Plan on three board feet per shelf.

Photocopy the templates in Figure B, p. 118, then transfer the pattern to your blanks with a hot iron (Photo 1).

Making the parts

Lay out the shelf pieces on your wood (Photo 2). If you're thinking of making several shelves at once, stack up to three of your blanks using 1/2-in.-square pieces of double-stick tape. Be careful when taking the stacked pieces apart after sawing because the double-stick tape is strong enough to take some wood with it. To avoid any problem, dribble some mineral spirits between the layers to dissolve the adhesive before separating them.

Cut out the shelf parts on a scroll saw (Photo 3). Finish-sand all your pieces before assembly. It's a lot easier to sand flat pieces now rather than trying to get into a bunch of small corners later. Begin with 120-grit paper and work your way up to 320-grit.

Putting it all together

For maximum strength, the brackets (C in Figure A, p. 118) are held onto the wall panel (B in Figure A) with screws. Nails are used to fasten the shelf (A in Figure A) to the brackets because their holes are easily filled. Take care when nailing, drilling or driving screws because the shelf parts are thin and delicate. Use a light touch to prevent splits.

Assembly is an exercise in small-part management. Trying to do without clamps may seem quicker, but you'd have to be built like an octopus to pull it off. The entire assembly can be done with the wall panel lying flat on your bench and using a simple 2x4 as a clamping aid. Here's how:

1. Square up the edges of a 2x4 and cut to 7-5/8 in., then clamp the brackets to the ends of the 2x4 (Photo 4).

2. Use a tape measure to center the brackets on the back of the wall panel, then mark their location (Photo 4).

3. Turn the wall panel over and center the bracket assembly on the face of the back panel. Place the shelf on your bench so that one bracket overhangs the edge (Photo 5).

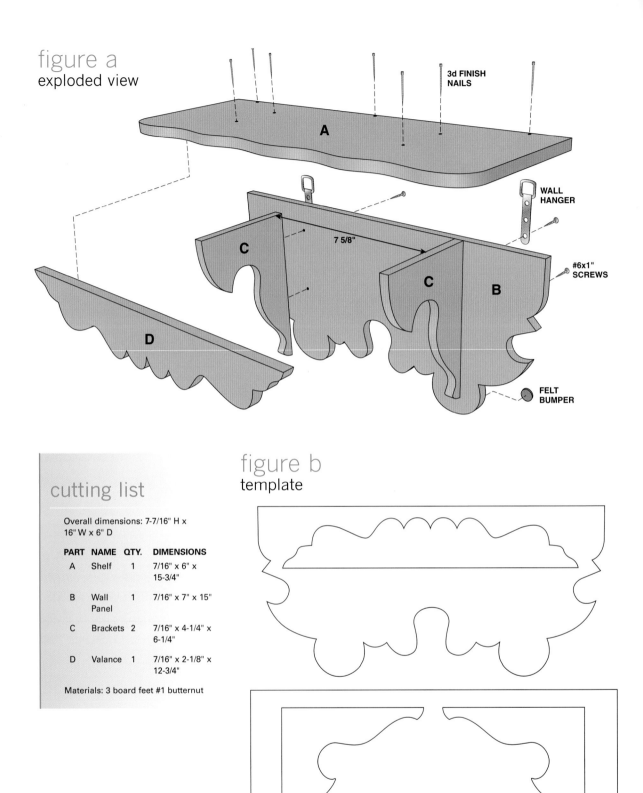

figure a
exploded view

A

3d FINISH NAILS

WALL HANGER

7 5/8"

C

C

B

#6x1" SCREWS

D

FELT BUMPER

cutting list

Overall dimensions: 7-7/16" H x 16" W x 6" D

PART	NAME	QTY.	DIMENSIONS
A	Shelf	1	7/16" x 6" x 15-3/4"
B	Wall Panel	1	7/16" x 7" x 15"
C	Brackets	2	7/16" x 4-1/4" x 6-1/4"
D	Valance	1	7/16" x 2-1/8" x 12-3/4"

Materials: 3 board feet #1 butternut

figure b
template

Make a photocopy of these templates at 200 percent enlargement (you'll need a copier that handles 11 x 17-in. paper). Then, take the enlargement and cover one of the images with a piece of white paper and photocopy again at 200 percent (400 percent total enlargement). Remove the paper, cover the other image and photocopy. Set the tone scale as dark as it can go without causing gray shadows on the white background. This will ensure a heavy coat of toner for transferring onto your template stock.

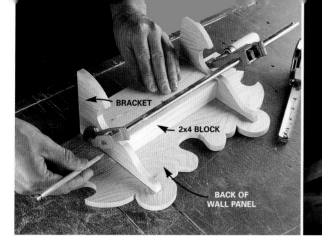

4 Outline the shelf brackets onto the back of the wall panel. This will show you exactly where to drill the pilot holes for the screws.

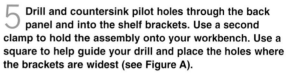

5 Drill and countersink pilot holes through the back panel and into the shelf brackets. Use a second clamp to hold the assembly onto your workbench. Use a square to help guide your drill and place the holes where the brackets are widest (see Figure A).

4. Drill two 3/32-in. pilot holes and fasten with two #6 x 1-in. screws (Photo 5). To avoid stripping out the holes, drive the screws by hand.

5. Turn the piece around and repeat step 4 for the other bracket.

6. Slide the wall panel assembly back onto your bench. Center the shelf, top-side down, on the brackets. Then, trace the bracket's outline onto the shelf.

7. Turn the shelf right-side up and re-center the brackets. Then, use a clamp to secure the shelf to the 2x4 block (Photo 6).

8. Use the bracket outlines as a guide and drill two 1/16-in. pilot holes through the shelf into each bracket. Be sure to place the holes where the brackets are wide enough to accept the screw. Drill three holes along the back edge of the shelf for nailing the top to the wall panel.

9. Run a small bead of glue along the top edge of the back panel and nail the top to the brackets and wall panel (Photo 6).

10. Attach the valance (Photo 7).

Finishing touches

Use 320-grit sandpaper to do a little touch-up sanding and ease the edges. Now you're ready to finish. Watco medium walnut oil was used for the finish and Behlen Fil-Sticks were used to fill the nail holes.

Now, attach a couple wall hangers to the back and you're ready to hang your shelf! You just need to find the perfect spot, "… a little to your left … a little lower …"

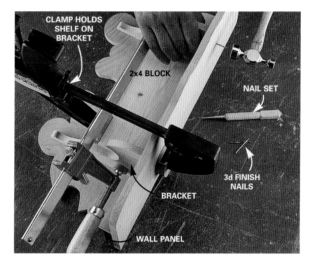

6 Nail the top to the brackets with 3d finish nails. Use a small hammer and tap (don't drive) the nail into the bracket. Use a nail set to countersink the nail heads.

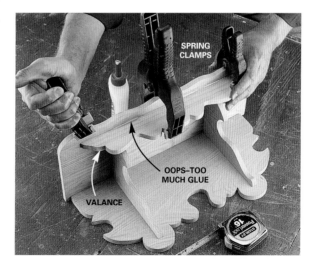

7 Clamp the valance onto the underside of the top with spring clamps. Use a thin bead of glue to minimize squeeze out. A damp cloth can be used to wipe away any excess glue before it sets.

Swedish wall shelves **119**

Floating shelves– hollow door

Strong, quick to build and no visible supports

These "floating" shelves are perfect for displaying your collectibles, photos, travel mementos or just about anything. Without the brackets and clunky hardware you'd find with store-bought shelves or kits, they seem to be suspended in midair.

These shelves are strong, too. While they're not designed to hold your old set of Encyclopaedia Britannicas, they're certainly capable of it. No one would believe that they're made from plain, old lightweight and inexpensive hollow-core doors.

In this article, you'll learn how to install these shelves (and shorter ones) securely with basic tools. Even if you think you have no DIY skills you can tackle this project.

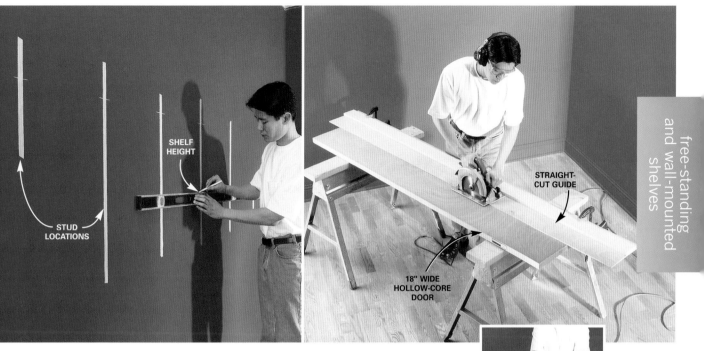

1 Trace the horizontal location for each shelf using a 4-ft. level as your guide. Use a stud finder to mark the locations of the studs and lightly press masking tape over each one. If you don't have a string line, use a long straightedge and mark the wall with a pencil. Check your marks with the 4-ft. level.

2 Cut the door blank lengthwise after clamping a straightedge guide to the door. Be sure to use a 40-tooth carbide blade for a smooth cut.

Surprise—a low-cost project that requires only basic tools

Each shelf is made from half of an 18-in. hollow-core door, which costs $18. That's only about $9 a shelf, plus the minimal cost of the lag screws (Photo 4) and cleat that hold the shelf to the wall. You can buy new hollow-core interior doors at a home center or lumberyard (just be sure the door doesn't have predrilled holes for locksets). You may find only 24-in.-wide doors, but the door can be any width; just try to minimize the waste. And you might be able to get doors free from yard sales or other sources.

As far as tools go, you can get by with just a circular saw and edge guide (Photo 2) to cut the door. However, it's recommended that you use a table saw to cut the cleat because a clean, straight cut is important for a good-looking shelf. (If you don't own a table saw, use a friend's or have the cleat cut at a full-service lumberyard.) You'll also need a stud finder, a chisel, a hammer, a wrench, 1-in. brads, 3-1/2-in. lag screws, carpenter's glue and a level.

making it fit your space

Build shorter shelves by cutting the shelf to length. Glue a filler block flush with the end and nail each side with small brad nails.

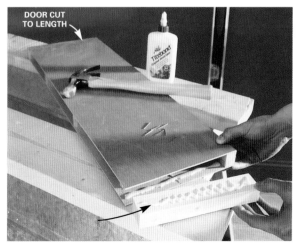

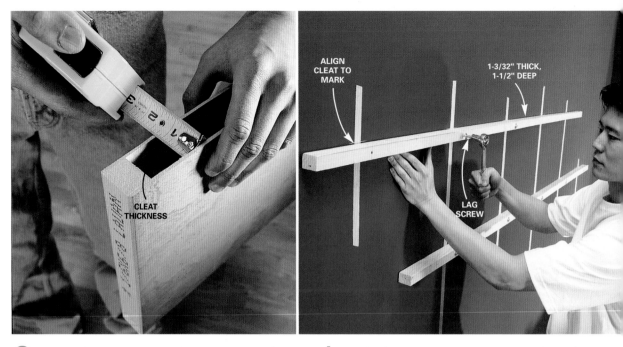

3 Measure the space between the outer veneers of the door and cut cleats from a 2x4 to this thickness. Our measurement was 1-3/32 inch. Use straight, dry lumber for cleats.

4 Predrill 1/4-in.-dia. holes at the stud locations after you cut the cleats to length (the measurement between the end blocks of the door half). Hold the cleat to your line on the wall and drill into the stud with a 1/8-in. bit. Using a wrench, install one lag screw into each stud until it's tight. Use 1/4-in. x 3-1/2 in. lag screws. Each cleat must be straight as an arrow.

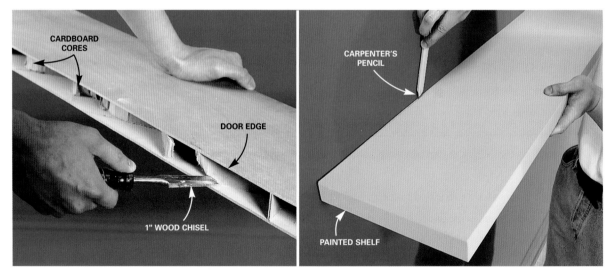

5 Cut away the corrugated cardboard cores at least 1-1/2 in. from the cut edge. Scrape away the glue carefully without gouging the wood surface.

6 Dry-fit the shelf to make sure the blank fits over the cleat. Check the back side of the shelf and scribe it to the wall if necessary. Use a block plane or sander to remove material from the back edge for a tight fit.

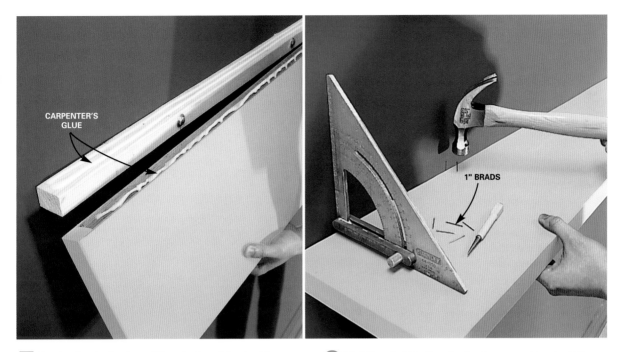

CARPENTER'S
GLUE

1" BRADS

7 Apply glue to the top of the cleat and the inside bottom edge of the door blank. Slide the shelf over the wood cleat.

8 Nail the shelf to the cleat using a square as your guide. Start at the middle and work your way to each end. Use 1-in. brad nails spaced 8 in. apart.

If you want a different look . . .

We chose to paint our shelves, but if you want the beauty of real wood, you can buy the door in wood veneers like oak or maple (ours was lauan). If you decide on a natural wood finish, you'll need to cover the exposed edges with a matching wood trim. If you go this route, first shave off 1/8 in. from the front and side edges with a table saw to eliminate the slight bevel on each edge, then apply the matching trim. You can also cover the entire shelf with plastic laminate if you want a tough, hard-surfaced shelf.

You may want to change the depth of your shelves as well. Don't exceed 9 in. or you'll start to weaken the cantilever strength of the shelf. Feel free to make narrower or shorter shelves, as shown on p. 121.

Handy Hints®

Use a needle-nose pliers or Popsicle stick with a split end to hold the 1-in. brads while nailing.

Create a rock-hard finish with a low-gloss enamel paint

The whole job will go a lot smoother if you paint the shelves before you install them. If you intend to paint the room, also do that before you install the shelves because it's a drag to cut around each shelf with a paint brush. Just be sure to sand your wood door with 150-grit sandpaper before you paint. If the surface is still rough and porous after sanding, fill the pores by applying a paste wood filler (like Elmer's wood filler) with a 3-in. drywall knife. Let it dry and sand the surface again.

These shelves are permanent—they're tough to remove!

The glue not only makes the shelves strong but also impossible to remove without ruining them. You'll have to cut them in place 2 in. away from the wall with a circular saw to expose the lag screws and then remove the cleats with a wrench. That's unfortunate, but you can always make another set cheaply and easily.

Portable bookshelf

Here's a cool knock-down shelf for a dorm room or den. You just slide the shelves between the dowels, and they pinch the shelves to stiffen the bookshelf. It works great if you're careful about two things:

- Make the space between the dowel holes exactly 1/16 in. wider than the thickness of the shelf board.
- Be sure the shelf thickness is the same from end to end and side to side.

After test-fitting a dowel in a trial hole (you want a tight fit), drill holes in a jig board so the space between the holes is your shelf thickness plus 1/16 inch. Clamp the jig board on the ends of the legs and drill the holes. Cut the dowels 1-3/4 in. longer than the shelf width, then dry assemble (no glue). Mark the angled ends of the legs parallel to the shelves and cut off the tips to make the legs sit flat. Disassemble and glue the dowels in the leg holes. When the glue dries, slide the shelves in and load them up.

Cutting List
Perfectly flat 1x12 lumber or plywood
2 shelves: 11-1/4 in. wide x 3 ft. long
4 risers: 2-1/4 in. wide x 24 in. long
8 dowels: 3/4 in. dia. x 13 in. long

DOWEL

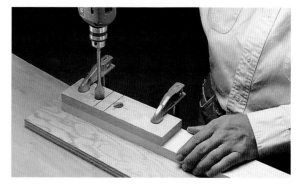

Easy-to-build display shelving

Assemble this simple shelf from 1x4s and tempered glass. Fasten the side boards to the 4-ft. back sections with carpenter's glue and 6d finish nails. Paint the brackets and screw them to wall studs. Buy round-cornered tempered glass shelves and slide them into place.

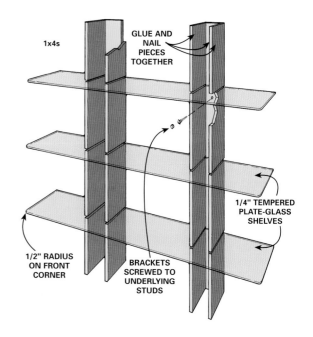

1x4s

GLUE AND NAIL PIECES TOGETHER

1/4" TEMPERED PLATE-GLASS SHELVES

1/2" RADIUS ON FRONT CORNER

BRACKETS SCREWED TO UNDERLYING STUDS

Closet rod and shelf

This project will save you hours of ironing and organiz- ing. Now you can hang up your shirts and jackets as soon as they're out of the dryer—no more wrinkled shirts at the bottom of the basket. You'll also gain an out-of-the-way upper shelf to store all sorts of supplies and other odds and ends.

Just go to your home center and get standard closet rod brackets, a closet rod and a precut 12-in.-deep Melamine shelf (all for about $25). Also pick up some dry- wall anchors, or if you have concrete, some plastic anchors and a corresponding masonry bit. Follow the instructions in Photos 1 and 2.

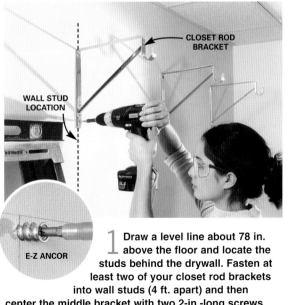

CLOSET ROD BRACKET

WALL STUD LOCATION

E-Z ANCOR

1 Draw a level line about 78 in. above the floor and locate the studs behind the drywall. Fasten at least two of your closet rod brackets into wall studs (4 ft. apart) and then center the middle bracket with two 2-in.-long screws into wall anchors (inset).

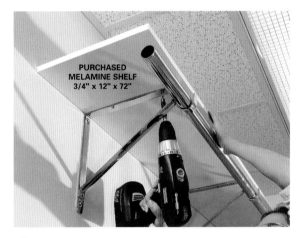

PURCHASED MELAMINE SHELF 3/4" x 12" x 72"

2 Fasten your 12-in.-deep Melamine shelf onto the tops of the brackets with 1/2-in. screws. Next, insert your closet rod, drill 1/8-in. holes into the rod, and secure it to the brackets with No. 6 x 1/2-in. sheet metal screws.

Free-form wall shelves

Here's a shelf that allows for a creative, one-of-a-kind edge treatment. Hung on the wall without any visible means of support, these shelves are real eye catchers.

Choose boards that are at least 1-1/4 in. thick and no more than about 7 in. wide. Wood with wane, bark pockets or end checks are perfect candidates. (You guessed it—this is a great way to use reject boards that are just too pretty to throw away or burn.)

First, true up the top and back edge with a hand plane or jointer. The back edge of the board is planed a degree or two less than perpendicular to keep objects from rolling off the shelf. Next, position the keyhole hangers out toward the ends of the shelves. Try to space the hangers every 16 in. so the shelves can be mounted directly to wall studs. The keyholes are mounted either horizontally or vertically and placed near the top edge to provide a bearing surface below the attachment point. Mark the profile of the hangers with a sharp knife and carefully chisel out the mortises to the exact depth of the hangers. Next, drill a recess at the bottom of each mortise (approx. 5/16 in. deep) to allow the wall-mounted screws to securely engage the hangers.

Now you're ready to shape the rest of the shelf. The gently curved and beveled ends can be cut on a bandsaw. Don't think too hard about how each piece should look. You can have good results by simply letting the grain figure determine the shape of the shelf. Just remove the loose or broken stuff and smooth out any rough edges with a carver's gouge.

Finish with a couple coats of oil, hang it up and you've got a conversation piece that will wow your houseguests.

figure a
wall mount

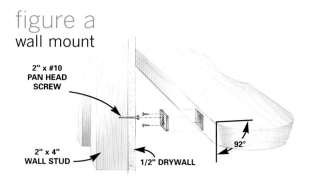

2" x #10
PAN HEAD
SCREW

2" x 4"
WALL STUD

1/2" DRYWALL

92°

Stud stuffer

Transform a bare wall space into an attractive storage shelf. This shelf fits anywhere between studs (behind a door for example) spaced 16-in. on center. Build the box as tall as you want. (It could be a broom closet!) Use 14-1/4-in.-wide, 1x4 boards screwed together at each corner with 1-5/8-in. drywall screws. Frame the box with trim that matches other trim in the room. Nail and glue on a 1/4-in.-thick plywood back. Cut out the hole in your wall. Screw or nail the box to the studs through the sides of the box. You can finish yours off with a 1x4 shelf.

NAIL HERE

Petite shelves

Turn a single 3-ft.-long, 1x12 hardwood board into small shelves to organize a desktop or counter. Cut off a 15-in.-long board for the shelves, rip it in the middle to make two shelves, and cut 45-degree bevels on the two long front edges with a router or table saw. Bevel the ends of the other board, cut dadoes crosswise (cut a dado on scrap and test fit the shelves first!) and rip it into four narrower boards, two at 1-3/8 in. wide and two at 4 in. wide. Finish, then assemble with brass screws and finish washers.

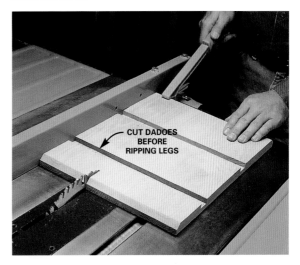

CUT DADOES BEFORE RIPPING LEGS

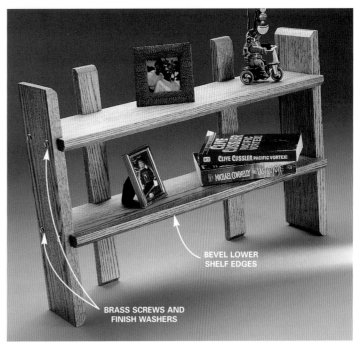

BEVEL LOWER SHELF EDGES

BRASS SCREWS AND FINISH WASHERS

section 5

built-in shelves & bookcases

Cherry bookcase........................130

Floor-to-ceiling bookcases.....140

Handy Hints® 151

Gallery of ideas 152

Cherry bookcase

This bookcase features simple pocket screw joints and a modular design you can adapt to any room

Some bookcases have plenty of charm but are shy on actual shelf space. Others will house stacks of books but are short on looks. This elegant design does it all, featuring more than 43 ft. of shelf space.

This multicomponent system has two 7-ft.-tall end bookcases plus a shorter center cabinet with glass doors to create dust-free storage for electronics or your favorite collectibles. The total width is just over 10 ft., but you can build narrower or wider individual components to custom-size it to fit nearly any room. You can build the system into a corner as shown, center it along a wall, or if you like, build it wall to wall. The total cost was about $1,500.

Don't confuse this project's elegance with complexity. The step-by-step building process is well within an intermediate skill level. As far as special tools go, a portable table saw is a must. The flat homemade moldings and dentils are simply cut from 3/4-in.-thick boards. The face frame and door joints are made with an inexpensive pocket hole jig and can be assembled in minutes. Even if you've never used a jig like this, it only takes about 15 minutes to get up to speed on it. A power miter saw also is a real timesaver. And either buying or renting an air-powered finish nailer and compressor will save even more time and get better results.

Cherry isn't available at home centers. You'll need to find a specialty hardwood lumber supplier that stocks cherry boards and plywood. If cherry isn't available in your area, consider another hardwood like oak, maple or birch.

project at a glance

skill level
intermediate

tools
pocket screw jig
circular saw
drill
bar clamps
finish nailer
belt sander
table saw

cost
about $1,500

Start with simple boxes

Cut the plywood for the sides, top and bottom to width on your table saw. You'll notice in the Cutting List (p. 132) that the outer plywood sides (E) are 1/4 in. wider than the inner plywood sides (A). This additional width covers the 1/4-in. plywood back nailed to the back of the inner sides so that you'll get a nice, right-to-the-wall look when viewed from the side.

Drill the shelf support holes into the inner sides using a homemade jig like the one shown in Photo 2. It takes a bit of work to make this simple jig, but you'll find tons of uses for it in the shop. The jig will ensure that each row of the shelf bracket holes will be level with each other. Don't bother drilling holes within the top and bottom foot of the sides, since they'll never be used that high or low; see Figure A, p. 133, for hole placement.

Screw the sides to the top and the bottom panels (Photo 3) with 1-3/4-in. wood screws. Next cut your 1/4-in. plywood back to the dimensions in the Cutting List. Use the factory edges of the plywood back to square up the cabinet as you nail it to the backsides of parts A and B.

Thicken the box sides for function as well as looks

The bookcases don't need to have double-thick side walls, but thick walls look more substantial and keep books from being hidden behind the wide face frame front.

With the simple box completed, add straight 2x2s to the sides as shown in Photo 4. Apply yellow wood glue to the edge and hold it firmly against the side of the box as

you nail it with your nail gun from inside the box. Use 1-1/2-in. nails. Be sure the front 2x2 is flush with the inner side (A) and the outer side (E). The back 2x2 is best placed slightly in from the back edge of the outer side so it won't keep the cabinet away from the wall as you screw it in place later.

Once you glue and nail the outer plywood sides to the 2x2s (Photo 4), cut the cabinet top to the dimensions in the Cutting List. If you're customizing the cabinets to a different size, cut this top piece 2-1/4 in. deeper and 3-1/2 in. wider than the outer dimensions of the top of each cabinet assembly.

Now ask somebody to help you carry these two cabinet boxes into your room and get ready to tip them up into place. Be sure you've removed the baseboard around the bookcase location, and save the pieces so you can recut them to fit against the bookcase sides once you've finished the job.

A pocket hole jig helps join the face and door frames

If you've ever butt-joined two pieces of wood with dowels or biscuits, you'll surely appreciate the speed and strength of pocket hole joinery. Unlike dowel and biscuit assembly, there's no messy glue or clamps. Just set the jig on the backside of the rail (top or bottom horizontal piece), squeeze the locking plate pliers, drill the holes, remove the jig and then drive the screws through the angle

shopping list

DESCRIPTION	QTY.
3/4" cherry plywood	5
1/4" cherry plywood	2
1x4 x 7' cherry	12
1x6 x 8' cherry	5
1x8 x 8' cherry	1
Door hinges	2 pr.
3/16" tempered door glass (measure to fit)	2
Magnetic door catches	2
Yellow wood glue	1 pt.
Door glass retainers	12
No. 4 brass screws	12
1/4" shelf supports	44
Pneumatic gun nails (3/4, 1-1/4, 1-1/2")	
1-1/4" wood screws, box of 100	1
1-3/4" wood screws, box of 100	1
Epoxy glue	1
Cherry finish	2 qts.

cutting list

KEY	PCS.	SIZE & DESCRIPTION
A	4	3/4" x 11-5/8" x 84" inner plywood cabinet sides
B	4	3/4" x 11-5/8" x 33" plywood cabinet top, bottom
C	2	1/4" x 34-1/2" x 83" plywood cabinet backs
D	8	1-1/2" x 1-1/2" x 84" pine
E	4	3/4" x 11-7/8" x 84" outer plywood cabinet sides
F	2	3/4" x 14-1/8" x 42-1/2" plywood cabinet tops
G	4	3/4" x 1-1/2" x 33" upper and lower fastening strips
H1	2	3/4" x 7-1/4" x 32-1/2" face frame arch
H2	2	3/4" x 5-1/2" x 32-1/2" face frame base
J	4	3/4" x 3-1/2" x 84" face frame sides
K1	2	3/4" x 5-1/2" x 40" center cabinet side wings
K2	4	3/4" x 1-1/2" x 11-7/8" cabinet cleats

cutting list continued

KEY	PCS.	SIZE & DESCRIPTION
K3	2	3/4" x 1-1/2" x 40-1/2" wall cleats
L1	1	3/4" x 17-3/8" x 42" plywood center cabinet floor*
L2	1	3/4" x 11-7/8" x 42" plywood center cabinet shelf*
M	2	3/4" x 3-1/2" x 40" center face frame sides
N1	1	3/4" x 3" x 35" center face frame top
N2	1	3/4" x 5-1/2" x 35" center face frame base
P	1	3/4" x 19-5/8" x 45" plywood center cabinet top*
Q1	4	1/4" x 2-1/4" x 11-7/8" cabinet side fillets
Q2	2	1/4" x 2-1/4" x 4-3/4" cabinet side fillets
R1	32	3/4" x 3-1/6" x 2-1/4" dentils
R2	28	3/4" x 1-1/2" x 3-1/16" dentil spacers
R3	16'	3/4" x 1" upper molding
R4	16'	3/4" x 1" top molding
S	4	3/4" x 2-1/4" x 31-1/2" door stiles
T1	2	3/4" x 7-1/4" x 12-15/16" arched door rails
T2	2	3/4" x 3" x 12-15/16" bottom door rails
U	17'	3/16" x 3/4" glass edging*
V	10	3/4" x 11" x 32-13/16" plywood shelves
W1	10	1/2" x 1-1/4" x 32-13/16" shelf nosing
W2	1	1/2" x 1-1/4" x 40" shelf nosing
X	5'	5/8" x 5/8" door muntins*

* Cut to fit

figure a
bookcase details

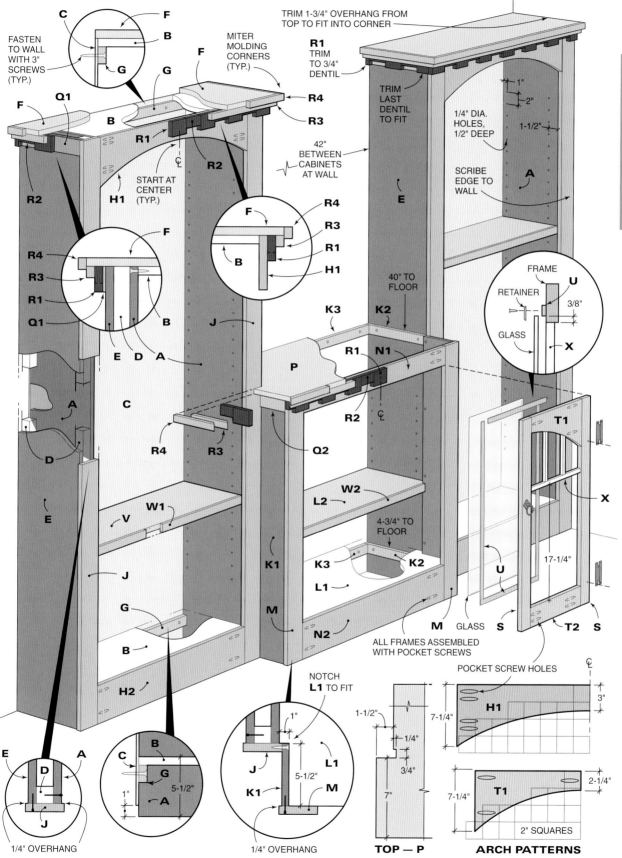

FASTEN TO WALL WITH 3" SCREWS (TYP.)

C

F

B

G

Q1

F

F

B

R1

R2

R2

H1

START AT CENTER (TYP.)

R4

R3

R1

Q1

B

E D A

A

C

D

E

R4

R3

J

W1

V

J

G

B

H2

MITER MOLDING CORNERS (TYP.)

R4

R3

F

R4

R3

R1

B

H1

J

TRIM 1-3/4" OVERHANG FROM TOP TO FIT INTO CORNER

R1 TRIM TO 3/4" DENTIL

TRIM LAST DENTIL TO FIT

42" BETWEEN CABINETS AT WALL

E

40" TO FLOOR

K3

K2

P

R1

N1

R2

Q2

R4

R3

K1

M

N2

W2

L2

K3

L1

K2

4-3/4" TO FLOOR

ALL FRAMES ASSEMBLED WITH POCKET SCREWS

1/4" DIA. HOLES, 1/2" DEEP

1"

2"

1-1/2"

SCRIBE EDGE TO WALL

A

FRAME

RETAINER

GLASS

U

3/8"

X

T1

X

U

M GLASS

S

T2

S

E

A

D

J

1/4" OVERHANG

B

C

G

A

5-1/2"

1"

1/4" OVERHANG

NOTCH **L1** TO FIT

1"

J

K1

L1

M

5-1/2"

1-1/2"

1/4"

3/4"

7"

TOP — P

POCKET SCREW HOLES

H1

3"

7-1/4"

T1

2-1/4"

7-1/4"

2" SQUARES

ARCH PATTERNS

1 Cut 3/4-in. plywood sides and tops using your circular saw and a cutting guide. Support your workpiece with 2x4s beneath to keep the cut from buckling and pinching the blade.

SQUARE CUTTING GUIDE

2x4 SUPPORTS

2 Make a drilling guide jig for the shelf supports from 1/8-in.-thick steel. Drill holes every 2 in. and carefully place the jig on each panel (A) for uniformly spaced holes 1/2 in. deep. Use a stop block to control the depth (photo below). See Figure A for positioning details.

STOP BLOCK

A

SHELF PIN HOLE GUIDE

---

pilot holes into the face frame sides. You'll be amazed at the strength of the joints and how flush the surfaces align. For the best results, be sure you hold the two pieces you are joining down firmly on a clean, flat surface so the screw drives precisely for perfect alignment. You can also refer back to the entryway pocket screw shelf project on p. 106 for more advice.

1/4" BRAD POINT BIT

STOP BLOCK

DEPTH STOP

Cut the curves for the top rails of the face frames and the door frames using your jigsaw and the pattern shown in Figure A. Clamp the cut piece to the side of your workbench or sawhorse and then use your belt sander to carefully smooth the irregularities of your cut. Then just cut the lower rails to length with your miter saw and pocket-screw them together as shown in Photos 6 and 7.

Plumb and install the side bookcases

Chances are your walls and floor have some irregularity like a corner that's not exactly square or a wall slightly out of whack. Start with the corner cabinet and get it reasonably plumb and level with shims. Close is good enough because the project design is somewhat forgiving. Leave about a 1/8-in. gap between the side wall and the cabinet to make room for your face frame to overhang a bit. Screw the corner cabinet to the wall (Photo 9).

Once the first cabinet is set, draw a plumb line 42 in. away from this cabinet. Slide the next wall cabinet over to this line and shim it to be perfectly level with the first cabinet. Screw the cabinet to the wall, through the fastening strips at the top and bottom, and into the wall studs.

With the tall side cabinets securely fastened, bring the face frames into the room and check their fit against the faces of the wall cabinets. If you're installing one of the cabinets against the side wall, you may need to scribe and trim the face frame a bit before you install it (Photo 10). Trim or sand, if necessary, and then apply glue to the front of each cabinet and nail each face frame assembly in place with your finish nailer (Photo 11).

Build the center cabinet in place

Unlike the flanking side cabinets that you build in your shop area, the center cabinet relies on the outer cabinets for part of its structure, so it needs to be built right in the room. Cut the flanking side wing pieces (K1), align them with the edges of the face frames, drill a pilot hole and screw them in place as shown in Photo 12. Next cut the support strips (K2 and K3) and screw them to the cabinet sides and back wall as supports for the center cabinet floor and top (Photo 13). Cut and notch the floor piece (L1) and nail it to the cleats. Next, position the center face frame over the side wings,

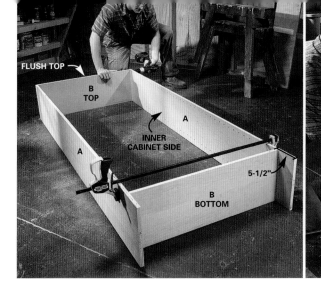

3 Predrill and screw the inner side panels (A) to the top and bottom (B) with 1-3/4-in. wood screws. Nail the 1/4-in. plywood back to the inner side panels and the top and bottom to square up the box.

4 Glue and nail the 2x2 spacers to the sides from inside the box with your nail gun. Complete the cabinet box by gluing and nailing the outer plywood panels to the 2x2. Glue and nail fastening strips (G) in place at this time.

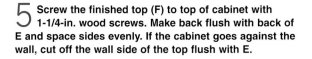

5 Screw the finished top (F) to top of cabinet with 1-1/4-in. wood screws. Make back flush with back of E and space sides evenly. If the cabinet goes against the wall, cut off the wall side of the top flush with E.

6 Cut the arched curves with a jigsaw, smooth them with a belt sander, then drill the backside of the arched front using a pocket hole jig.

leaving a 1/4-in. overhang on each side. Then glue and nail it (1-1/2-in. nails) to the wings (K1) and to the front edge of the plywood floor (Photo 14).

Be sure to cut the top (P) so it projects 1-3/4 in. past each side wing (K1) and 1-1/2 in. out from the face frame in the front. If the top projects a bit farther than this, all the better, since you can sand it flush with the upper molding strip (R3) later. This way you'll be sure that the top strip (R4) will fit against the plywood top.

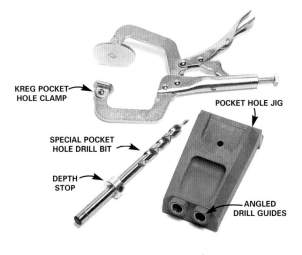

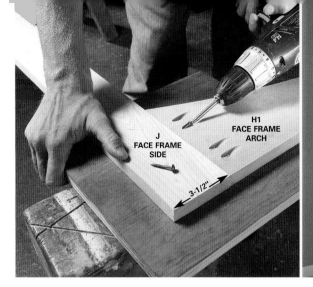

7 Hold the sides of the frame so the edges are flush and drive the screws into the mating piece with special pocket hole screws. This makes for a superstrong, fast, glue-free joint.

8 Set the cabinet boxes in the room. Space them 42 in. apart. Shim as necessary to get them both plumb and level. Cover spaces or gaps at the bottom with base shoe molding later.

9 Locate the studs and screw the cabinet through the horizontal fastening strip into the wall.

10 Scribe the preassembled face frame to the side wall if your wall is uneven. Make sure the face frame overlaps the inner panel by 1/4 in. on each side.

Mass-produce the dentils and spacers ahead of time

Just rip a 1x4 board to 3-1/16 in. on your table saw and another to 1-1/2 in. wide. Mark a line on your miter saw to cut the wider board into 2-1/4-in. lengths to make the dentils. Change the mark to cut the narrower board into 3-1/16-in. lengths to make the spacers. Next, rip a couple of 1x4 boards to 1-in. widths to make the upper moldings R3 and R4.

Mark the top center of each cabinet, then grab three dentils and mark the center bottom of each. Align the marks and nail the dentils smack in the middle of the cabinets up against the projecting plywood tops. Next, nail a spacer on each side and work your way to the side of each side cabinet. Nail a 1/4-in. x 2-1/4-in. fillet on the side of each cabinet to fur out the dentil moldings to keep them aligned. Measure and cut this piece carefully so it ends up flush with the overhanging face frame. *NOTE:* Make the

11 Center the second face frame assembly on the box, mark it, then glue and nail it to the front of the cabinet.

12 Screw the side wings (K1) of the center cabinet to the edges of the face frames of the side cabinets. Drill pilot holes and use 1-1/4-in. wood screws. Be sure they're perfectly plumb and level with each other.

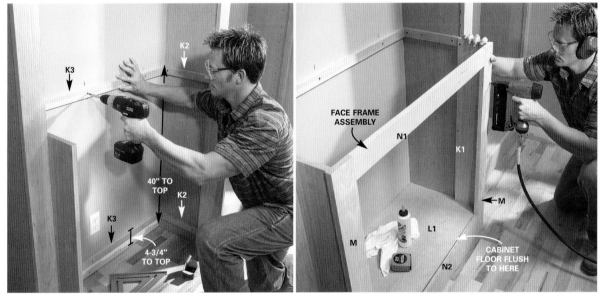

13 Level and screw the cleats (K2 and K3) to the cabinet sides and wall studs with wood screws (1-1/4-in. screws on the sides and 2-1/2-in. screws into the wall studs).

14 Cut and nail the center cabinet floor (L1) to the lower cleats, then glue and nail the center face frame assembly to the side wings (K1) and floor (L1). Then cut and nail on the top (P).

dentils visually equal at the corners (Photo 15). To achieve this, trim the side corner 3/4 in. less than the front corner dentil.

To finish the top cornice of each bookcase, cut the molding strips to length on your miter saw and nail them with 1-1/2-in. nails. After the first strip is in place, check the overhang of each top. The top edge should be flush with the face of R3. If the pieces aren't flush, sand them flush with a belt sander.

Get the spacing right on inset doors

Inset doors are often considered difficult to install because they have to fit precisely inside the face frame. First, cut the pieces, then assemble each door using your pocket hole jig. Next, clamp the doors together at their center stiles with spacers between them and set the assembly up to your opening (Photo 17). You may need to trim an edge or two with your table saw, and for fine adjustments, use your belt sander.

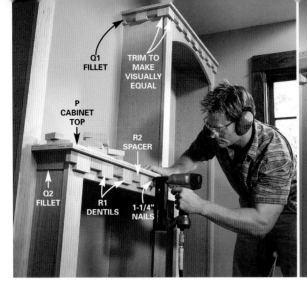

15 Mark the center of each cabinet. Center the first dentil (R1) over the mark and then nail the dentil spacers (R2) between each pair of dentils. Use 1-1/4-in. brads in your nail gun. Trim the dentils at the corners to ensure even wraps around each side of the corner.

16 Miter the ends of the upper trim strips R3 and R4 and nail the first strip to the dentils and the upper strip to the cabinet top.

17 Cut the door stiles (S) and the door rails (T1 and T2) and assemble them with pocket holes and screws as shown in Figure A. Trim the doors and set the top and side clearance. Use tablet backer cardboard from a legal pad for spacers. Use double spacers at the top, bottom and center and use single spacers at the sides against the face frame. Install the face-mount hinges and magnetic catches at this time.

18 Cut 3/16-in. glass edging strips from 3/4-in.-thick material, then glue and tack them (5/8-in. brads) to the inside of the door. Leave a 3/8-in. lip for the tempered glass panels.

To hang the door, use simple face-mount hinges. Just shim the doors as shown and then drill pilot holes holding the hinge in place. Work in one screw at a time to get perfect hinge placement. Once the doors are mounted, remove the hinges until after finishing.

Shaping a recess for glass along the inside of the door can be a hassle, so to keep things simple, a much easier method than routing it out is shown (Photo 18). All you need to do is cut strips and glue and nail them to the backside of the door. Leave a 3/8-in. lip for the glass to sit on and then buy simple glass retainers at a hardware store. Then order the glass. Get tempered

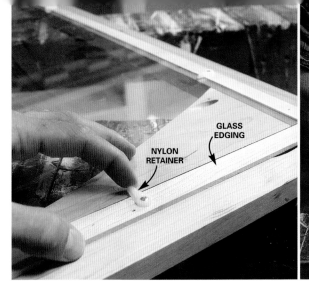

19 Buy nylon storm window glass retainers from a hardware store along with No. 4 brass screws to secure the glass.

NYLON RETAINER

GLASS EDGING

20 Cut muntin strips on your table saw and glue them to the ends of the rails and stiles with epoxy. Be careful not to slop glue on the wood faces or it will block your finish stain.

EPOXY GLUE

MUNTINS

glass from a glass supplier because regular double-strength glass is prone to breaking.

The final step to great-looking doors is to make the muntins that overlay the glass (Photo 20). Measure up 17-1/4 in. from the bottom of the door glass opening and then measure, cut and place the first horizontal piece so the bottom edge of it aligns with the mark. Mark these strips so you'll get three equal glass sections. Cut angles on the tops to follow your curve. Once you're happy with how they fit, mark the muntin placement onto the door, mix up some clear epoxy (Photo 20) and glue the assembly to itself and the door edge. *NOTE:* Place wax paper under joints to keep the epoxy off the glass. Once the glue is set, clean up any excess at the joints with a file or sandpaper.

Cut the shelves from 3/4-in. plywood and add edging

Rip the plywood and then cut it to length (3/16 in. less than the inside measure) for the shelf blanks. To give the

making it fit your space

Trying to decide where to install your shelves? First make sure your ceiling height is adequate and there's enough wall space. You can change the dimensions of the project a bit to accommodate your space. Second, check the locations of your electrical receptacles. Make sure they don't fall directly behind one of the cabinet sides. If they do, adjust the placement of the cabinets or move the receptacle.

If the receptacle is directly behind one of the tall cabinets, you'll need to cut an opening in the back of the cabinet to expose the receptacle and install a box extender. If you need help, consult a licensed electrician. Ductwork may also need to be extended.

shelves a solid wood look, rip strips 1-1/4 in. wide and then 1/2 in. thick. Cut them the same length as the shelf blanks and glue and nail them to cover the plywood edge.

The center shelf is made the same way. Just rip the plywood to 11-7/8 in. wide and cut the solid edge strip and nail it in place so the strip falls between the inside faces of the side wings (K1). You'll also need to drill holes into the center cabinet sides for the shelf supports.

Cherry can be a fussy wood to finish

To help get the cherry finish as even as possible, use pre-finish wood conditioner first and then apply the color. This will cut down on the blotchiness, and sanding lightly over trouble spots will give you a good look. After three days, apply satin polyurethane for a nice, even, durable sheen. If you hate fussy finishing, apply a clear oil or varnish and the cherry will darken naturally with age.

Floor-to-ceiling bookcases

Designed to fit, even if your room isn't perfectly square

The classic Greek Revival styling of this library is reminiscent of bookcases built more than a hundred years ago. The bookcases look ornate but are relatively simple to build. There's no complex joinery like mortise-and-tenon, or even doweling, so if you've hung a new door or trimmed a room with new molding, you have the expertise to handle this project.

The bookcases are sized to fit into a typical room with an 8-ft. ceiling and at least 8 ft. of wall space. It's perfect for something like a typical bedroom that you want to convert to a library or home office. It can also be expanded by adding standards (the upright partitions; see Figure B, p. 143).

This project has been engineered to work even if your room is a bit out of kilter. The moldings are applied after the main standards are installed to cover any gaps resulting from uneven floors or walls.

project at a glance

skill level
intermediate to advanced

tools
circular saw
drill
power miter saw
table saw
belt sander
clamps
level
framing square

cost
about $1,400

On p. 142, you'll find a list of the materials you'll need to complete this project. For a project the size of the one shown here, expect to spend about $600 on materials. The optional ladder and hardware will cost an additional $800 or more. And even though this project isn't complicated, it's still going to take you at least 40 hours to build.

Planning ahead

As you plan, note the location of your electrical receptacles and heating ducts. They may dictate where you place the standards. Your only other absolute is that the ladder support rod (Photo 17) should not span more than 36 in. between brackets.

Use a level to check for irregularities like a sloping floor or an uneven wall. If your walls and floor aren't exactly straight or level, you'll be able to scribe the standards on the back side and bottom, and then cut along your scribe for a perfect fit.

If you decide to include the ladder in your design, be aware that it could take up to five weeks for delivery. This shouldn't slow you down—you can get started with the project and install the ladder when it arrives.

These bookcases were built onto a wood floor. If you have carpeting, you'll need to pull back the carpet and pad and reinstall them later around the base of the bookcases. And yes, the ladder will roll on carpeting as well.

figure a
casings and moldings

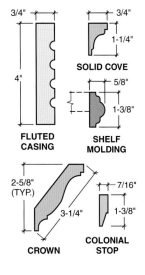

SOLID COVE — 3/4", 3/4", 1-1/4"

FLUTED CASING — 4", 3/4"

SHELF MOLDING — 5/8", 1-3/8"

CROWN — 2-5/8" (TYP.), 3-1/4"

COLONIAL STOP — 7/16", 1-3/8"

Getting started

You don't need a fancy shop to cut the plywood and build the standards. A set of sawhorses under a sheet of 3/4-in. plywood will work just fine. The first order of business is to rip (cut lengthwise) the eight pieces of plywood 13-3/4 in. wide to make the standards. You can use a table saw, but you may prefer to use a circular saw and a homemade rip guide, made from two pieces of straight scrap plywood (see Photo 2 for more information).

After ripping the pieces, you'll need to crosscut the tops to length as shown in Photo 3. The length will be the measurement from your floor to the ceiling minus 1 inch. This extra inch of space is needed to slide the bookcase top (C) into position later (Photo 12).

After cutting the plywood to size, you'll need to drill 1/4-in.-dia. holes into the inner sides for the shelf support hardware. These holes must be

shopping List

ITEM	QTY.
3/4" x 4' x 8' birch plywood	5
2x4 x 8' pine	8
1x2 x 10' pine	1
1x4 x 10' maple board	1
7/16" x 1-1/2" x 10' colonial stop	2
7/16" x 1-1/2" x 8' colonial stop	6
1-1/16" x 4-1/2" x 8" plinth blocks	4
3/4" x 4" x 7' fluted casing	4
5/8" x 1-1/2" x 8' shelf molding	7
1-1/4" x 8' cove molding	1
3-1/4" x 10' crown molding	1
1/4" peg-style shelf brackets	84
1-1/4" x 1/8" x 6' flat steel	1
1-1/2" x 1-1/2" brass angle with screws	12
Carpenter's glue	1 qt.
3/4" x 17-gauge nails	1 pkg.
1-1/4" x 17-gauge brads	1 pkg.
4d, 6d and 8d finish nails	1 lb. each
Wood conditioner	2 qts.
Pecan stain	2 qts.
Satin polyurethane	2 qts.
Colored putty stick	1
7-ft. rolling ladder and hardware	1

cutting list

KEY	QTY.	SIZE & DESCRIPTION
A	3	3/4" x 13-3/4" x 96" plywood (trim to fit)
A1	3	3/4" x 13-3/4" x 96" plywood (trim to fit)
A2	2	3/4" x 13-3/4" x 96" plywood (trim to fit)
B	8	1-1/2" x 3-1/2" x 96" pine
C	1	3/4" x 13-3/4" x 96" plywood (trim to fit)
D	1	7/16" x 1-3/8" x 10' maple colonial stop (cut into dentils)
D1	1	7/16" x 1-3/8" x 10' maple colonial stop (cut to fit)
D2	1	3/4" x 3-1/2" x 10' maple dentil backer board
E	6	7/16" x 1-3/8" x 8' maple colonial stop (cut to fit)
F	4	1-1/16" x 4-1/2" x 8" maple plinth blocks
G	4	3/4" x 4" x 7' maple fluted casing (cut to fit)
H	1	1-1/4" x 8' maple cove molding (cut to fit each column)
J	1	3-1/4" x 10' maple crown molding
K	7	3/4" x 11-3/8" x 32" plywood (trim to fit)
L	14	3/4" x 11-3/8" x 26" plywood (trim to fit)
M	7	5/8" x 1-3/8" x 32" shelf molding
M1	14	5/8" x 1-3/8" x 26" shelf molding

figure b
bookcase details

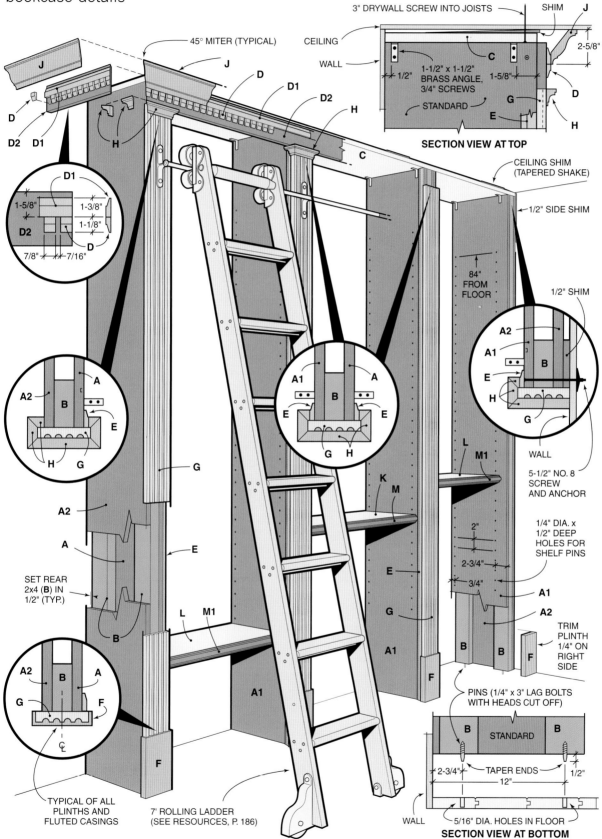

J

45° MITER (TYPICAL)

J

D

D1

D2

H

D

D2 D1

H

3" DRYWALL SCREW INTO JOISTS

SHIM

J

CEILING

WALL

C

**1-1/2" x 1-1/2"
BRASS ANGLE,
3/4" SCREWS**

1/2"

1-5/8"

2-5/8"

D

G

STANDARD

E

H

SECTION VIEW AT TOP

D1

1-5/8"

1-3/8"

1-1/8"

D2

D

7/8"

7/16"

H

C

**CEILING SHIM
(TAPERED SHAKE)**

1/2" SIDE SHIM

**84"
FROM
FLOOR**

1/2" SHIM

A2

A1

B

E

H

G

WALL

**5-1/2" NO. 8
SCREW
AND ANCHOR**

A

A2

B

E

H

G

A1

A

B

E

E

G

H

A2

A

E

**SET REAR
2x4 (B) IN
1/2" (TYP.)**

B

G

L

M1

K

M

E

G

A1

L

M1

A1

A2

A

G

F

CL

**TYPICAL OF ALL
PLINTHS AND
FLUTED CASINGS**

**7' ROLLING LADDER
(SEE RESOURCES, P. 186)**

F

**1/4" DIA. x
1/2" DEEP
HOLES FOR
SHELF PINS**

2"

2-3/4"

3/4"

A1

A2

**TRIM
PLINTH
1/4" ON
RIGHT
SIDE**

F

B

B

F

**PINS (1/4" x 3" LAG BOLTS
WITH HEADS CUT OFF)**

B

STANDARD

B

2-3/4"

TAPER ENDS

1/2"

12"

WALL

5/16" DIA. HOLES IN FLOOR

SECTION VIEW AT BOTTOM

USE SHORTEST
HEIGHT FOR
MEASUREMENT

3/4" VENEERED
PLYWOOD

HOMEMADE
JIG

13-3/4"

RIPPING MARK

1 Measure the height and width of your wall. Note the locations of all receptacles, switches and vents. They may require you to modify the design.

2 Rip the 3/4-in. plywood into the 13-3/4-in. strips you'll later use to construct each of the four standards. You'll need to rip eight identical pieces (see Figure B) for
the standards and one for the top (C).

precise from one standard to the next so your shelves don't wobble. The best way to ensure this is to make a drilling jig.

To make your drilling jig, buy a 1-1/4-in. x 1/8-in. x 6-ft. piece of mild steel from your hardware store. Mark it every 2 in. from one end to the other as shown in Photo 4. Next mark centers 3/4 in. from the edge. To keep your bit from wandering as you drill, use a center punch to dent the steel at your mark. Using a 1/4-in. high-speed steel twist bit, drill all the holes. Sand off sharp burrs with 100-grit sandpaper.

To finish your jig, drill four 1/16-in. holes evenly spaced along its length so you can tack it to the plywood sides (Photo 5).

TIP: Mark the jig with a bit of paint so the top can be identified at a glance. If you don't, you can easily flip it end for end and then get the shelf-hole pattern goofed up!

making it fit your space

As you can see, the center section of our bookcases is 6 in. wider than the two outer sections. This establishes a focal point, and the two side sections provide symmetry. However, this exact design may not work for your room. To check, carefully measure your selected site. Take into consideration the height, width and any obstructions unique to your room. You may find you need to alter these plans a bit. Keep in mind, you can move the standards closer together or add another standard or two to fit a longer wall.

At 84 in. from the bottom, mark each plywood piece (A, A1) for drilling. The A2 pieces don't get drilled. Align the top hole of the jig with your mark. Align the edge of the jig with the back edge of the plywood (Photo 5). Nail the jig to the workpiece with 3/4-in.-long, 17-gauge nails.

To get clean, flat-bottomed holes, use a 1/4-in. brad point bit in your drill. Use a stop collar on the bit to ensure a 1/2-in. depth, and drill into each hole of the jig.

Drill the front holes next, centered at 2-3/4 in. from the front edge as shown in Figure B. *NOTE:* Pieces A and A1 are mirror images of each other, so double-check to make sure you drill them correctly.

Sandwich-gluing the standards

Now you're ready to glue the plywood pieces (A, A1, A2)

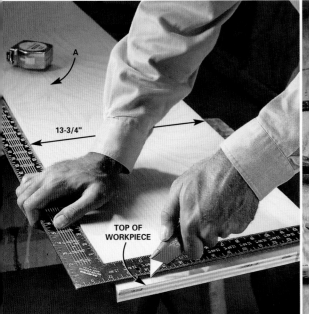

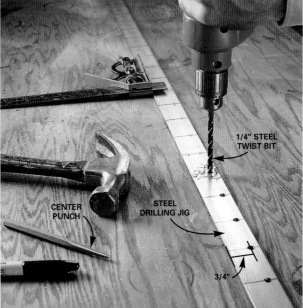

3 Score the 3/4-in. plywood with a sharp utility knife at a height 1 in. shorter than your floor-to-ceiling measurement in Photo 1. Crosscut along the edge of the scored line to get a splinter-free cut.

4 Make a jig to drill accurate holes for the shelf-support hardware. Drill 1/4-in.-dia. holes 2 in. apart and centered 3/4 in. from the edge into a 1-1/4-in. x 1/8-in. x 6-ft. piece of mild steel.

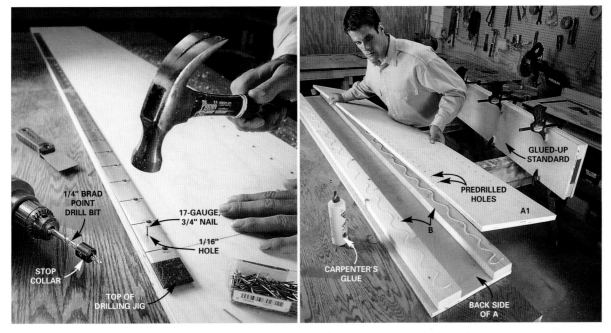

5 Nail the jig (use 3/4-in. nails) to the plywood pieces (A and A1) you've already cut. The jig needs four 1/16-in. holes along its length for the small 3/4-in. nails that attach it to the plywood (see Figure B). Once the jig is secure to the plywood piece, drill 1/4-in. holes 1/2 in. deep through each of the jig holes into the plywood. *NOTE:* The two outside end panels (A2) do not have holes drilled into them.

6 Glue the 2x4s between the plywood pieces (A and A1) "sandwich style" to create the two middle upright standards. Also, glue together an A2 and A1 for the far right standard and an A and an A2 for the far left standard. After gluing, clamp them for at least two hours. Be sure the front 2x4 (B) is flush with the front side of the panels and the rear 2x4 (B) is set in about 1/2 inch. The extra 1/2 in. on the back makes scribing to the wall much easier.

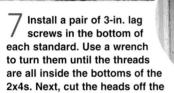

7 Install a pair of 3-in. lag screws in the bottom of each standard. Use a wrench to turn them until the threads are all inside the bottoms of the 2x4s. Next, cut the heads off the screws with a hacksaw and file a slight taper on the bottom of the protruding screw shaft. These pins will hold the standards into holes in the floor (to be drilled later).

8 Glue the dentil pieces (D) to the 1x4 backer board (D2), using masking tape to hold them as the glue dries. Parts D, D1 and D2 must be prestained before gluing. Allow the stain to dry at least a day so the glue will stick. The dentils are made from colonial-style stop that is first ripped to 1-1/8 in. then cut to 7/8-in. lengths. The filler piece at the top is the same uncut stop with the detailed side up. This piece will be hidden by the crown molding (J) later.

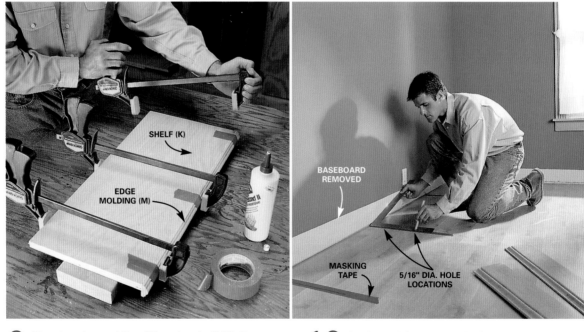

9 Glue the edge molding (M) to the shelf (K). Use masking tape to align the molding and clamp it until the glue sets.

10 Apply masking tape to the floor where the standards will be placed, then mark the hole locations for the pins (cut-off screws). Use a framing square as a guide to ensure that the holes will be perpendicular to the wall. Be sure to remove the baseboard.

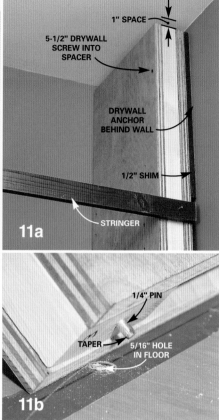

11a

11b

11 Tip the standards into position, making sure the 1/4-in. pins fall into the 5/16-in. holes. The standard against the corner wall is spaced 1/2 in. away from the wall and is secured at the top front with a 5-1/2-in. drywall screw driven into a drywall anchor. The screw and anchor will hold the first piece in position while the temporary stringers will hold the rest of the standards parallel. Nail the temporary stringers to each standard, making sure the top width measurement equals the bottom width measurement.

and the 2x4s (B) that make each standard. To make sure you glue the correct sides (A, A1, A2) together, study Figure B. Cut the 2x4s to the same length as the plywood. Spread the glue (about a 1/4-in. bead in a squiggly pattern) on both sides of the 2x4s and place them onto the plywood (Photo 6). Recess the rear 2x4 about 1/2 in. from the back. If your wall is uneven, this will make it much easier to scribe it to the wall later on. **TIP:** To keep the pieces from drifting as you clamp them, drive a finish nail through the plywood into the 2x4 to hold it in position. Set this nail just below the surface and fill the hole later.

Once the glue has set overnight, position each standard in your room to see how each one fits against the floor and the wall. A gap of 1/8 in. at places against the wall is fine; if the gap is any larger, the standard should be scribed to fit. If you live in an old house that's settled considerably, check for a gap on the floor as someone holds each standard

against the wall. If there's a gap at the front, scribe the standard to the floor and sand to your mark with a belt sander (or random orbital sander). If you make any adjustments to the standards, mark them in the order you'll install them—1, 2, 3 and so on.

Installing the pins

The pins that secure the standards to the floor are nothing more than 1/4-in. x 3-in. lag screws with their heads cut off with a hacksaw. Carefully mark the hole centers as shown

figure c
hole locations for pins (top view)

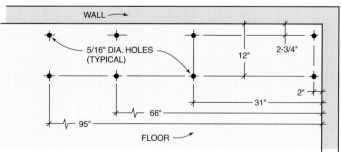

CABINET TOP (C)

STANDARDS

BRASS ANGLES

CROWN HEIGHT

DENTIL ASSEMBLY

CEILING SHIM

MITERED END

12 Slide the cabinet top (C) over the standards and secure it in place with brass angle hardware (Figure B) in the front and back of each standard. Be sure the standards are positioned and spaced properly before screwing the top in place. Once the top is secured to the standards, be sure the standards are against the wall. Then screw the top to the ceiling joists in three locations (two screws at each location), shimming the gaps (Photo 13) between the top and the ceiling with wood shims. *NOTE:* You may have to use a stud finder to locate the joists. Or install blocks between joists in the attic.

13 Miter the end of the dentil assembly, then cut it to length. Nail the assembly to the front of the standards with 6d finish nails. The 2-5/8-in. distance from the ceiling to the top of the dentil is critical. The bottom of the crown molding profile needs to align with the top of the dentils (Photo 16).

in Figure B, then predrill a 3/16-in. hole. Turn the lag screws into the holes with an end wrench, leaving 1/2 in. of the shaft exposed (Photo 7). Now, cut the heads off the screws and file a slight taper near the end to help guide the pins into the holes you'll be drilling into the floor later.

Making the dentil molding

The dentils (D) are made from colonial stop molding (also called Princeton style; Figure A, p. 142). First, rip off the square side so the stop is 1-1/8 in. wide (if you don't own a table saw, have this done at the lumberyard). Now cut the molding into 7/8-in.-long pieces to make each dentil. It's slow going but the finished look is worth it. Use a power miter saw to cut the lengths (you can rent one for about $45 a day). The filler piece (D1) at the top side of the dentils (D) is the same molding with the square side toward the top of the dentil as shown in Photo 8. The backer board (D2) is 1x4 maple.

Nail the filler (D1) to the backer board using 1-1/4-in. brads every 6 inches. Then glue the dentil pieces to D2 as shown in Photo 8, using just enough glue so it doesn't ooze from the sides of the dentils. Let this piece sit for 24 hours before handling it.

Making the shelves

It's recommended you cut the shelves at the same time as the standards (see Cutting List, p. 142). Cut the shelf fronts (M and M1) and glue them to the shelves (Photo 9). You can trim the completed shelves to exact length (the measurement between standards, minus 3/16 in.) when you're ready to install them. This way they can be prefinished along with the other pieces.

Prefinishing

It's a lot faster to stain and varnish in your shop than it is to painstakingly avoid spilling onto your walls and floor.

14 Nail the fluted casing fronts (use 6d finish nails) to the front edge of each standard after nailing the plinth blocks at the bottom. Also, be sure to nail the side trim (E) even with the fronts of the standards. Since the plinths are wider than the fluted casing, you'll need to rip 1/4 in. from the width of the plinth against the wall.

15 Nail the 1-1/4-in. cove molding (H) to the tops of the fluted casing. The cove molding should wrap around the sides of the fluted casing.

And you can confine the odor of the finish to your workshop or garage; just be sure your work area is at least 60 degrees F. After the bookcases are completely installed, you can touch up any cut ends with stain and fill nail holes with colored putty. For a blotch-free, even color on the birch, apply wood conditioner before the pecan stain. Use a polyurethane varnish for durability.

Installing the standards and top

Remove your baseboard where the bookcases will go. Pull the nails through from the backside with a pliers and set the baseboard aside. You'll reinstall it later between the standards. To help you see the pin-location marks for the standards, apply tape on the floor as shown in Photo 10. Next, carefully measure using Figure C, p. 147, as your guide. Use a square so your measurements will be perpendicular to the wall, and drill the 5/16-in.-dia. holes into the floor for the first standard (Figure C).

Space the first standard 1/2 in. from the side wall (Photo 11a). This will provide enough space for the fluted front casing (Photo 14) to overhang equal amounts on each side of the standard. To hold the top of the standard away from the wall (Photo 11a and Figure B), install a shim near the top as shown and secure the standard to the wall with a 5-1/2-in. drywall screw driven into a drywall anchor. Make sure the shim is thick enough so the standard is plumb (Photo 11a). Now cut temporary stringers from scrap 1x2, two pieces 32 in. long and one piece 36 in. long (Photo 11).

Drill the corresponding 5/16-in.-dia. holes for the second standard into the floor and set it in place (Photo 11b). Nail a 32-in. temporary stringer from the first unit to the second, making sure the standards are perfectly parallel.

Once all the standards are in place, slip the top (C) into position (Photo 12) between the standards and the ceiling. When the front edge of the top is even with the fronts

16 Set the nails after nailing the crown molding (J) into the filler strip (D2). Use 4d finish nails every 12 in. to nail the crown molding. Miter each end at the outside corner and butt the other ends against the wall.

17 Install the rolling ladder hardware to the face of the cabinet according to the manufacturer's instructions.

of the standards, screw it to the top of the standards (Figure B) with 3/4-in. screws and brass angles. Then shim it tight to the ceiling. To lock the bookcases into position, screw the top to the ceiling joists with 3-in. drywall screws, making sure the backs of the standards are against the wall. Use at least six screws to secure the top directly to the joists. You can now remove the temporary stringers.

Installing the trim

First, nail the dentil assembly to the standards as shown in Photo 13. It should be high enough that the crown molding, when installed, will just touch the top of the dentils (D). Our crown molding is 3-1/4 in. wide across its face, and its bottom edge sits 2-5/8 in. below the ceiling (Figure B).

Next, nail the colonial stop (Figure A) on each side of the standards (E in Figure B). Nail each piece in place with 4d finish nails every 12 in., aligning it with the front of each standard. After the stop is nailed, nail the plinth blocks (F) at the base of each standard using 8d finish

nails. To cover the exposed faces of the standards, nail the fluted casing (use 6d finish nails in pairs every 18 in.) to each standard (Photo 14). Fit it tightly between the plinth and the dentil assembly.

To give each fluted casing the look of a real column, glue and tack the cove molding (H), mitering the corners around each top (Photo 15). Now to finish the bookcase at the ceiling, miter the crown molding and nail it in place as shown in Photo 16. *NOTE:* To enhance the built-in look of the project, we continued the crown molding around the entire ceiling.

The ladder

The rolling ladder is a handsome addition to any library. You can purchase yours by mail (see Resources, p. 186) after sending a dimensioned sketch of your project. All the necessary hardware and very clear instructions are included. The ladder is a safety hazard for small children, so adult supervision is advised.

A flip-up side for your shop cart

A handy addition to your shop is a cart with a flip-up side. Build it from plywood, with strong hinges on the top edge, a track on the lower edge of the folding side, and a semicircular cutout at the bottom. Weight your cart with a bag of sand or concrete mix, so it doesn't tip over. To use this contraption, lift one corner of your plywood, slide it on the track (good side out) and wheel the cart to the front of your table saw. Lift the flip-up side, slide the plywood onto the top of the cart (the semicircular cutout lets you grasp the bottom edge of the sheet), and you're ready to feed it into the saw. No more awkward gyrations while trying to carry the plywood, flip it over, and then hold it steady when you try to line it up with the fence.

HINGE

CUTOUT

BALLAST

TRACK

The 12-foot plywood hauler

If you have to lug full sheets of plywood (or even worse, MDF) around your shop, a 12-ft. length of rope is one of the handiest tools you can have. Simply tie a loop in each end and you have a simple handle for your sheet stock. A bowline knot is shown here, but any knot that doesn't slip would do the trick. With the sheet leaning up against a wall, simply slip a loop under the bottom corners, lift the rope, and off you go. This works for drywall, too. (P.S. In this photo the happy woodworker is on the other side so you can see better, but normally you'd be on the same side as the rope, for easier lifting.)

Gallery of ideas
Four more well-designed built-in bookcase styles

< **Bookcase and mantel**
This combination fireplace surround and bookcase was inspired by the Craftsman movement of the early twentieth century. The tapered columns showcase the hearth and the lower height of the bookcases on each side helps keep the fireplace as the focal point. See Resources, p. 186, for more information.

> **Craftsman-style library**
This bookcase utilizes shelving and trim that can be purchased in standard widths and sizes. The project is structured around the vertical columns that can be built in the shop or garage, then set in place. Simple 1x4 bases help support the columns at the bottom and an oak plywood cap with brackets finishes off the top. See Resources, p. 186, for more information.

Classic built-in bookcase

Curved brackets, column-like partitions and crown molding give this book-case a sophisticated, classic feel, yet there's no tricky joinery involved and the plywood, hard-wood lumber and mold-ings are all available at well-stocked lumberyards and home centers. A gel stain gives the birch and maple materials an antique cherry wood appearance. See Resources, p. 186, for more information.

Mission oak bookshelves

This solid oak, built-in bookcase has plenty of room for openly display-ing books and collectibles, plus lots of hidden cabi-net space below. The spacing of the vertical columns can easily be adjusted to accommodate windows and different-sized rooms.

The paneled cabinet doors can be made with an ordinary table saw, and the face frames and other parts are held together with an easy-to-use pocket hole screw jig. The columns and many other parts can be pre-built in your shop or garage. See Resources, p. 186, for more information.

section 6

offices and entertainment centers

Low-cost TV cabinet 156

Afternoon projects

   Sliding bookend 165

   Portable music box 165

Family message center..........166

Stackable shelves 174

Desktop file holder 181

Gallery of ideas 182

Low-cost TV cabinet

Simple joinery makes it fast—plywood makes it inexpensive

The striking style of this cabinet was inspired by visits to upscale furniture stores where similar pieces can be found selling for $1,500 or more. This unit was designed so you can build and finish it in about three weekends for a cost of less than $300! That will leave you more money for what you put inside the cabinet.

Design features

- The TV space is 39 in. wide by 30-1/2 in. tall by 23-3/4 in. deep, and will accommodate most 36-in. TVs, but measure your TV before building this cabinet.
- The two large component openings will accommodate stacks of high-tech TV gear. Each one measures 19-1/8 in. wide by 11-1/4 in. tall by 23-3/4 in. deep.
- Cutouts in the back of the TV shelf make it easy to run wires between the TV and the components.
- Two deep drawers provide lots of room for videotapes, DVDs or video-game junk.
- To create the bold color contrast, you can stain the stiles and top with a dye before assembly.

Tools and materials

This project requires a jigsaw, table saw and router. You'll also need a dado set for your table saw, a pattern bit for your router and clamps with a reach of at least 25 inches.

It takes only three sheets of 3/4-in.-thick plywood, one sheet of 1/4-in.-thick plywood and about 6 bd. ft. of lumber. Shop for plywood sheets that are similar in color and grain on at least one side, and be sure to face these sides out when you build your cabinet. The sheet of

project at a glance

skill level
intermediate

tools
jigsaw
table saw
router
clamps

cost
about $300

1/4-in. plywood for the back is less critical, since it will be almost totally hidden once you install your TV and components.

You can buy the birch plywood for this cabinet at most home centers, but you may have to sort through half the pile to find three sheets that are similar. It's easier to find matching plywood at a lumberyard. It will probably cost you more, but it may also save you some time and hassle.

You may need to buy the birch lumber from a lumberyard if your home center doesn't carry it.

Prepare the plywood parts

Cut out plywood parts A through G according to the Cutting List, p. 158, and Figure D, p. 161. Rough-cut your sheets of plywood into manageable sizes with a jigsaw or circular saw, and then do the final cutting on your table saw. Use a router and straightedge on parts that are too big for your table saw.

Edge band the plywood edges that will be visible when the project is complete (see Notes column in Cutting List). Pre-glued edge banding (see Resources, p. 186) is simple to apply with an old iron and easily trimmed with a utility knife (Photos 1 and 2). Rubbing the banding with a wood block helps it adhere to the plywood edge.

Screw the cabinet half of the drawer slides to the drawer divider and sides (F). It's easier to attach the slides now with the parts flat and before the cabinet is all assembled (Photo 3). Use ball-bearing slides with a weight rating of 100 pounds. Glue and clamp the rails (L) to the front edge of the bottom and sub top (C). Cut out the

wiring slots in the TV shelf (D) with a jigsaw.

Sand all of the plywood parts before moving on to assembly; 180-grit paper on an orbital sander is all it usually takes.

Assemble the inner drawer and component boxes

Screw together the upper and lower sections of the inner boxes separately (Photo 4). Then add the cleats (H) and join the two sections together (Photo 5). Use a 5/32-in. drill bit for pilot holes and a countersink bit for the screw heads. Be careful that you don't go too deep when drilling pilot holes.

Rabbet the sides and rout the feet

Rout the rabbet on the back edges of the sides (B) to accept the 1/4-in. plywood back. Stop the rabbet 4 in. from the sides' bottom.

Trace the foot profile on the bottom of the sides using the foot template (Figure B, p. 161). Rough-cut the foot detail with a jigsaw. Leave about 1/8 in. of extra material. Then trim this rough edge with a router and the template (Photo 6). You'll need a pattern bit for this routing.

File the inside corners at the top of the feet square, then edge band the exposed plywood edges around the foot opening. The edge banding will help protect the veneer on these edges from chipping due to bumps from shoes or a vacuum cleaner.

cutting list

Overall dimensions: 46-3/4" W x 27-3/4" D x 61" T

PART	ITEM	QTY	FINAL DIMENSIONS			NOTES
			T	W	L	
A	Top	1	3/4"	27-3/4"	46-3/4"	Edge band all four edges.
B	Sides	2	3/4"	24"	60-1/4"	
C	Bottom and sub top	2	3/4"	23"	40-1/2"	
D	TV/component shelves	2	3/4"	23-3/4"	40-1/2"	Edge band front edges.
E	Component sides/divider	3	3/4"	23-3/4"	11-1/4"	Edge band front edge of center divider only.
F	Drawer sides/divider	3	3/4"	23-3/4"	10"	Edge band front edge of center divider only.
G	Back	1	1/4"	41-1/2"	55-1/2"	Drill holes for power cords after assembled.
H	Cleats for inner box	6	3/4"	3/4"	20"	Miter front ends to make less visible when installed.
J	Bottom/sub top cleats	4	3/4"	3/4"	23"	
K	Long top cleat	1	3/4"	3/4"	38-1/2"	
L	Rails	2	3/4"	1-1/2"	40-1/2"	
M	Stiles	4	3/4"	2-1/2"*	60-1/4"	Tapered width is 2-3/8" at top and 1-5/8" at bottom.
N	Drawer fronts/backs	4	3/4"	8-1/2"*	16-5/8"*	Measure drawer opening to determine exact length.
P	Drawer sides	4	3/4"	8-1/2"	22"	
R	Drawer bottoms	2	1/4"	17-1/8"*	21"	Check width before gluing drawers together.
S	Drawer faces	2	3/4"	18-7/8"*	9-3/4"*	
T	Wood knobs	2	1-1/4" dia.			

*Approximate

NOTE: For information on toggle clamps, dye, drawer slides, edge banding and wood knobs, see Resources, p. 186.

personally speaking

Drilling a pilot hole is no time for guessing, especially when there's a risk of drilling too deep and going through the other side. To avoid this, mark the correct depth on the bit with a masking tape flag. When the flag gets close to the wood, slow down until it touches, and then stop drilling.

I got lucky on this drill-through. The bit pushed out the veneer, but it didn't break off. I was able to work some glue behind the veneer with a tiny nail and stick the veneer back in place. After the first coat of clear finish, I added a speck of matching wood filler for a near-perfect repair.

–Gary Wentz, editor
The Family Handyman

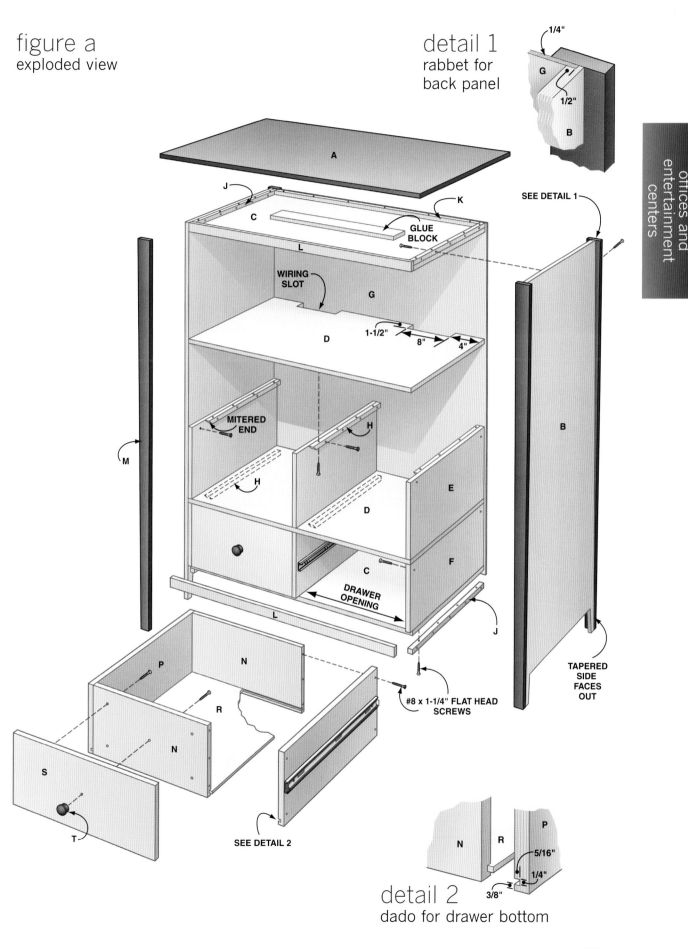

figure a
exploded view

detail 1
rabbet for back panel

1/4"

G

1/2"

B

A

J

C

GLUE BLOCK

L

K

SEE DETAIL 1

WIRING SLOT

G

D

1-1/2"

8"

4"

B

MITERED END

H

H

H

D

E

M

C

F

DRAWER OPENING

L

J

TAPERED SIDE FACES OUT

P

N

R

#8 x 1-1/4" FLAT HEAD SCREWS

N

S

T

SEE DETAIL 2

detail 2
dado for drawer bottom

N

R

P

5/16"

1/4"

3/8"

1 Iron on edge banding to cover the exposed edges of the uprights, shelves, top and drawers. A cheap or old iron works for this.

2 To trim the banding, set it on a flat surface and use a *sharp* utility knife. MDF or hardboard makes the best trimming surface because it has no grain. Wood grain can steer your knife off course.

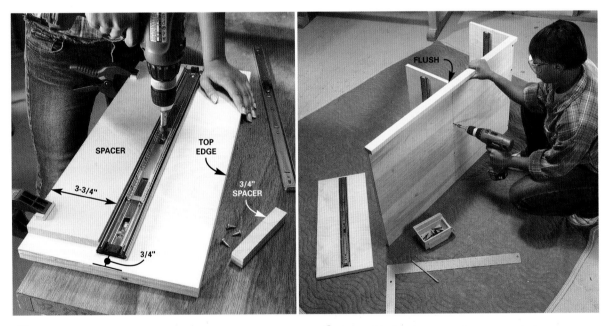

3 Screw the drawer slides onto the sides and center divider of the drawer section. It's easier to do it now while the parts are lying flat. A spacer makes centering the slides foolproof. Set the slides 3/4 in. back to allow for the inset drawer faces.

4 Assemble the drawer and component storage separately. Drill a pilot hole for each screw and make sure the front edges of the parts are flush.

Add the sides

Fasten the sides to the inner box assembly (Photo 7). They attach at the bottom with the cleats (J) and screws through the component and drawer section sides (E, F, Figure A, p. 159). The front edges of the sides (B) must be aligned flush with the front edge of these inner boxes. The back edges of the component and drawer sections should now align with the rabbet at the back of the sides.

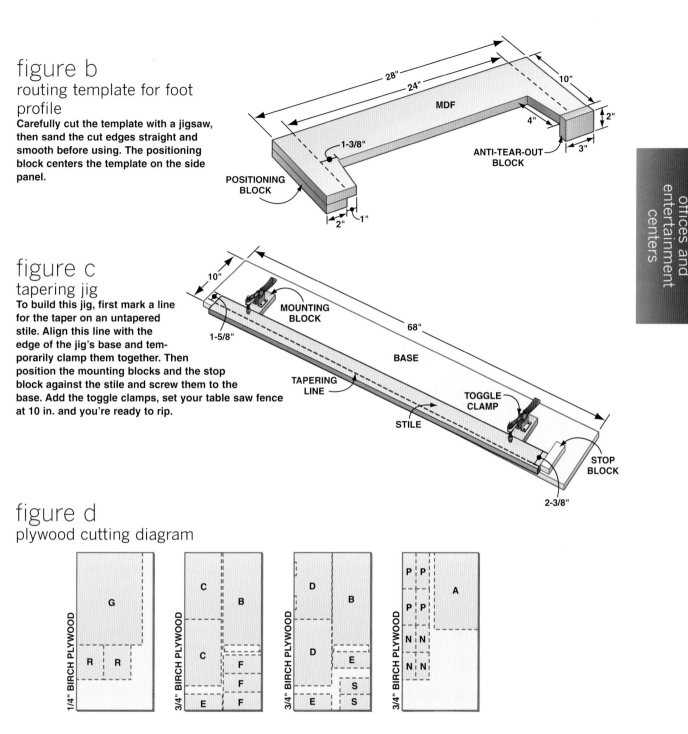

figure b
routing template for foot profile
Carefully cut the template with a jigsaw, then sand the cut edges straight and smooth before using. The positioning block centers the template on the side panel.

28"
24"
10"
MDF
1-3/8"
4"
2"
ANTI-TEAR-OUT BLOCK
3"
POSITIONING BLOCK
2" 1"

figure c
tapering jig
To build this jig, first mark a line for the taper on an untapered stile. Align this line with the edge of the jig's base and temporarily clamp them together. Then position the mounting blocks and the stop block against the stile and screw them to the base. Add the toggle clamps, set your table saw fence at 10 in. and you're ready to rip.

10"
1-5/8"
MOUNTING BLOCK
68"
BASE
TAPERING LINE
TOGGLE CLAMP
STILE
STOP BLOCK
2-3/8"

figure d
plywood cutting diagram

1/4" BIRCH PLYWOOD
G
R R

3/4" BIRCH PLYWOOD
C
B
C
F
F
E F

3/4" BIRCH PLYWOOD
D
B
D
E
E S

3/4" BIRCH PLYWOOD
P P
A
P P
N N
N N

Attach cleats (J, K) to the sub top. Then screw the sub top (C) to the sides. Stand the unit up and mark the location for the screws that will attach the back (G, Photo 8). Then lay the unit down and attach the back with screws every 6 in. (Photo 9).

Attach the stiles and the top
Build the stile-tapering jig (Figure C, above). You'll spend an hour making the jig, but it's worth it, because it makes quick and easy work of tapering the stiles (Photo 10). Before you remove each stile from the jig, label the tapered edge. This taper must face out when attached to the cabinet, and it's easy to mix up the tapered edge with the straight edge. Completely sand the stiles at this time.

Next stain the stiles, the top (A) and the drawer knobs (T). A dark brown alcohol-based dye stain was used for

5 Join the component section, which is simply a screwed-together plywood box, to the drawer section. The cleats keep the parts aligned.

6 Rough-cut the feet with a jigsaw and then trim the rough edge using a template and a pattern bit in your router. A small block glued to the right end of the template will prevent the plywood from tearing out at the end of the cut.

7 Screw the sides to the component and drawer sections from the inside. Fasten the cleat along the bottom edge. It should align flush with the foot opening.

8 Temporarily install the back panel with a couple of screws, but put it in backward. Then trace around the shelves and sides to show you where the screws should go when you turn the back around.

this cabinet. Dye stain is easy to work with, and it won't interfere with gluing.

Use 12 oz. of alcohol and add 1 oz. of dye. This makes a very dark dye solution, but that's what it took to get the wood as dark as that shown. Let the dye dry thoroughly before moving to the next step.

(If you plan to use an oil stain, skip the previous step. An oil stain will interfere with the gluing that takes place

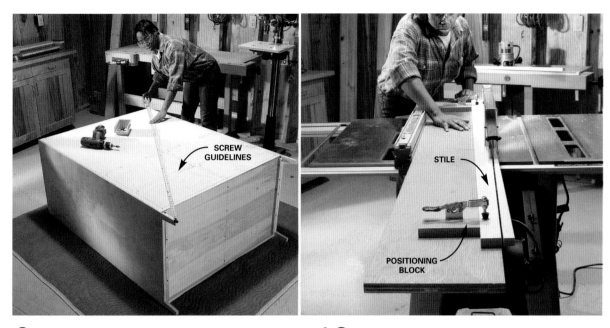

9 **Screw on the back. Begin by fastening one edge with a few screws. Then nudge the unit one way or the other until you get equal diagonal measurements, which means it's square. Then fasten the other edge, top, bottom and shelves with screws.**

SCREW GUIDELINES

10 **Taper the stiles that will be applied to the sides of the cabinet with a shop-made tapering jig. After sanding, stain the stiles.**

STILE

POSITIONING BLOCK

in Photos 11 and 12. Instead, wait until the front stiles and top are glued on. Then tape around them to keep stain off the rest of the cabinet.)

Glue the front stiles in place (Photo 11). Attach the rear stiles with screws. This allows you to remove them and the plywood back for easier finishing later on.

Glue the top in place (Photo 12). Don't use too much glue around the perimeter of the case; you want to avoid a squeeze-out mess. Masking tape is still a good idea to catch any drips. The top should overhang the front by 2-1/4 in., each side by 2-7/8 in. and the rear stiles by 3/4 inch. Use spacers to help center the top on the case. Once the top is aligned, weight it down and then immediately remove the spacers, or any squeezed-out glue might bond them to the top. Leave the weight on the top until the glue is dry.

Build and install the drawers

Cut out drawer parts N through R. Make the length of the drawer fronts and backs (N) so that when the drawers are assembled, they are 1 to 1-1/16 in. narrower than the width of the cabinet drawer opening (Figure A). This is the space required for most ball-bearing-type slides.

Cut dadoes in drawer parts N and P and then edge band the top edges of these parts. Sand these drawer box parts at this time.

Install the drawer bottoms (R) in the dadoes and assemble the drawer sides with glue and screws. Strips of masking tape along the joints will protect the sanded parts from glue squeeze-out. Wipe any glue squeeze-out off the tape, but leave the tape on until the glue in the joint has set up. Center the drawer half of the drawer slides on the outsides of the drawers and attach them with screws. Put the drawer boxes into the cabinet. Cut the drawer faces (S) 1/4 in. smaller than the drawer opening, and edge band all four edges. This will produce a clearance space around the sides of the drawer faces that is slightly less than 1/8 inch. Attach the drawer faces to the drawer boxes with screws (Photo 13).

Add the finishing touches

Seal the whole cabinet with spray-on shellac. The spray-on shellac will seal the dye stain, which will bleed and

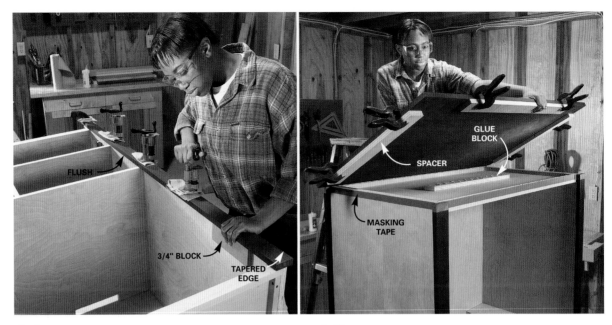

FLUSH

3/4" BLOCK

TAPERED EDGE

GLUE BLOCK

SPACER

MASKING TAPE

11 Glue and clamp the front stiles in place with the tapered edge facing out. Position the stiles flush with the inside of the drawer and components cabinet. Overhang the stile by 3/4 in. on the inside of the TV space.

12 Glue on the top. Spacers position it exactly, and masking tape catches any glue squeeze-out. A plywood glue block provides extra bonding area. Stack weights on the top and then remove the spacers before the glue dries.

13 Position inset drawer faces using spacers and drive a temporary screw though the center of the front, where the knob will be attached later. Then pull out the drawer and add screws from the inside.

14 Spray on a light coat of clear shellac. This seal coat keeps the dark dye stain from bleeding onto unstained wood areas and makes a good sealer for the polyurethane topcoat.

smear onto the unstained parts if you try to brush or wipe a finish over it. Use shellac in a well-ventilated area and wear a respirator with organic vapor cartridges. Lightly sand the shellac after it is completely dry and then topcoat the cabinet with a brush-on satin polyurethane varnish. Shellac makes a good seal coat, but polyurethane is a lot more durable.

Sliding bookend

To corral shelf-dwelling books or CDs that like to wander, cut 3/4-in.-thick hardwood pieces into 6-in. x 6-in. squares. Use a band saw or saber saw to cut a slot along one edge (with the grain) that's a smidgen wider than the shelf thickness. Stop the notch 3/4 in. from the other edge. Apply a finish to the bookend and slide it on the shelf.

offices and entertainment centers

Portable music box

Keep your portable CD player and CDs ready for use, but out of harm's way, with this sturdy case. This was designed to fit a specific CD player, and since yours may be different, measure it carefully and modify the dimensions accordingly. Cut 1/4-in.-thick walnut or other attractive plywood into sides, a bottom and a lid. Round the ends of the lid and bottom. Make three partitions out of 3/4-in.- to 1-in.-thick hardwood. Clamp the middle partition vertically in a drill press and carefully drill two 9/16-in. holes 4 in. deep in the upper end for spare batteries. With No. 6 brass screws (countersunk), secure the partitions to the bottom, then attach the sides. After sanding and finishing, put self-adhesive hook-and-loop fastener strips under the lid ends and the outside partition ends to hold the lid closed.

Cutting List
Sides: 14-1/2 in. x 6-1/2 in.
Top and Bottom: 14-3/4 in. x 2-1/2 in.
Partitions: 6 in. x 2-1/2 in.

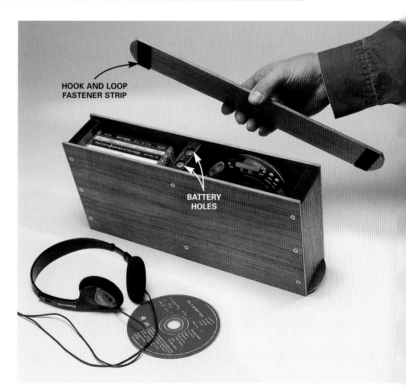

HOOK AND LOOP
FASTENER STRIP

BATTERY
HOLES

Family message center

This cabinet keeps everyone's schedule within easy reach ... without cluttering up the kitchen

Busy family? If you have trouble keeping track of the kids' or your spouse's schedule, and you want to make sure your messages are read, build this simple organizing cabinet. It has an erasable calendar for busy schedules and immediate messages; plenty of cork for photos, invitations, coupons and permission slips; a pull-down door with a notepad for short messages and shopping lists; and storage for a good supply of pens, postage stamps, tissue and other items that usually

clutter nearby table tops. It also has hooks for keys and shallow bins for magazines, mail, dog leashes, address books and homework (completed, no doubt).

This cabinet was designed to slip back into the wall between empty stud spaces, so you won't bump it as you go by and knock stuff off the board. And the closed doors keep most of the clutter out of sight.

You'll need a table saw, a miter saw and a pneumatic brad nailer for this project, in addition to standard hand tools, but you could also build the project with just a circular saw (with a cutting guide for straight cuts) and a drill.

Detective work comes first

Before cutting into the wall, try to get an idea of what's concealed inside it. Find stud locations with a stud finder or by tapping on the wall and listening for variations in tone. Be aware that blank walls can conceal a wide variety of framing—especially in older houses. *NOTE:* Locating studs in old plaster walls may require a more sensitive, higher-priced stud finder. If you absolutely can't find the studs, try removing a section of baseboard and opening the wall where you can hide the hole. Or tap a finish nail through the wall until you hit a stud, then measure over about 16 in. and tap the nail through again to find the next stud.

Once you've located studs, check both sides of the wall and the rooms above and below for heat registers, plumbing and electrical fixtures. If you find potential obstructions on adjacent floors, use an outside wall for a reference point to estimate if it'll obstruct your cabinet. Even if the location looks clear, you never know what's inside, so cut small holes in both cavities and double-check for obstructions. Cutting the hole with a utility knife is difficult, but it's safer than using a saw because you can keep the cuts shallow and away from any electrical wires (Photo 1). If you find obstructions, don't despair. Half of this message center is only 3/4 in. deep (not including trim). It may fit over the obstructions without any problem. Another option is to make the box shallower. You may also be able to extend wires around the boxes by rewiring, but consult an electrician or electrical inspector first.

making it fit your space

The message center fits inside a standard interior wall, which is usually constructed of 2x4s spaced 16 in. on center, with 14-1/2 in. of space between studs. Exterior walls won't work, because they have insulation in them. And some interior walls won't work either, if they have heating ducts, pipes and wiring running through them. You can easily adapt this project to any size and as many open cavities as you want. The basic concept is simple—just cut a hole in the drywall, insert a wooden box and add trim to it.

Cut the openings

Draw plumb lines at stud locations, then mark the rough opening height (34 in. from the floor to the bottom and 83 in. to the top). Adjust this height above the floor, if necessary, so the message center lines up with nearby door or window trim.

Check the studs for plumb (Photo 3) and adjust the box dimensions as needed to fit cleanly between them. In this situation, the center stud was plumb, but the left and right sides were out of plumb by 1/8 in. in opposite directions, so the two boxes were made 14-1/4 in. wide instead of 14-1/2 in. wide and left 1-5/8 in. between them. It's generally best to leave the center stud in place.

Build the boxes

This message center spans two stud cavities, with a deep side for shelves and miscellaneous storage and a shallow

figure a
message center details

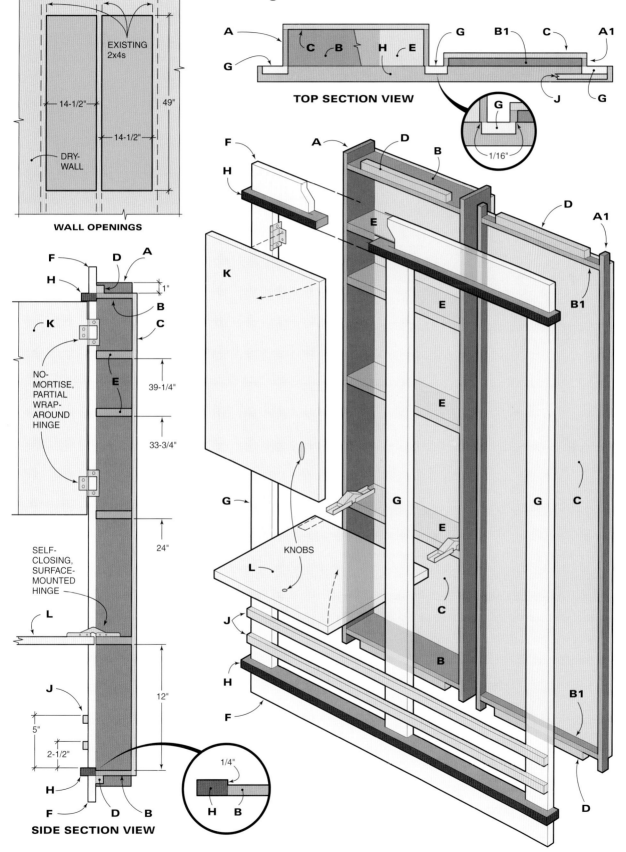

WALL OPENINGS

EXISTING
2x4s

14-1/2"

14-1/2"

49"

DRY-
WALL

TOP SECTION VIEW

A

C

B

H

E

G

B1

C

A1

G

G

J

G

1/16"

SIDE SECTION VIEW

F

D

A

H

B

K

C

E

NO-
MORTISE,
PARTIAL
WRAP-
AROUND
HINGE

39-1/4"

33-3/4"

24"

SELF-
CLOSING,
SURFACE-
MOUNTED
HINGE

L

J

12"

5"

2-1/2"

H

F

D

B

1/4"

H   B

1"

F

A

D

H

K

E

E

G

L

J

KNOBS

B

D

H

F

C

G

B1

B

B1

C

D

A1

G

E

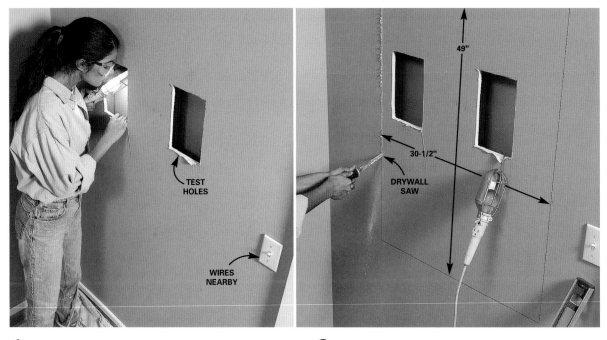

1 Find nearby studs with a stud finder, then cut a small opening with a utility knife in each stud cavity and check for obstructions. Save the cutouts in case you have to repair the wall.

2 Cut the opening to the desired height and size of your message center, following the studs with the drywall saw. Smooth ragged edges with a rasp or knife.

side for a cork message board and calendar. To maximize space, make the sides of the deep box from 1/2-in. birch plywood and the sides of the shallow message board from 1/2-in. x 3/4-in. pine. Nailing trim to a 1/2-in. edge is finicky work, so use a brad nailer or predrill the nail holes.

Cut the backs and side pieces from a 4 x 4-ft. sheet of 1/2-in. birch plywood using a table saw or a circular saw with an edge guide. If you use a circular saw, cut from the backside to avoid chipping the birch veneer. If possible, gang-cut pieces that are the same length (Photo 4). Use 1/2-in. plywood for the back for rigidity and give solid support for the cork board and any other items you want to mount.

Cut the long sides of the boxes 47-7/8 in. (A, A1, Figure A, p. 169), and nail the top and bottom pieces (B, B1) 1 in. in from the end to create nailer legs for the top and bottom trim pieces (F); see Photo 5. Glue and nail the back (C) down onto the box, aligning the edges and squaring the box as you nail (Photo 5). Tack down the back with 1-in. brad nails; longer nails might angle and break through the plywood sides. Use a damp cloth to wipe off any glue that oozes to the inside.

Install shelves

Nail the shelves (E) into place before joining the two boxes (Photo 6). Gang-cut the shelves from 1x4 pine, then slide them into position and hold them tight against square blocks of wood clamped to the sides. Mark the center of the shelf on the outside of the box frame to ensure accurate nailing (Photo 6). Use four 1-1/2-in. brads on each side and then flip the box over, connect the nailing lines from each side across the back and shoot a few brads in through the plywood back for extra strength and rigidity.

Join the boxes with the trim

Line the two boxes up with each other, then glue and nail the center trim (G) to join the sides, leaving a 1/16-in. reveal on each side. Center the center trim lengthwise to leave it about 1/4 in. short of each end. When you attach the top and bottom sills (H), this will give you a 1/4-in. lip to help keep papers and odds and ends from sliding out the bottom (Photo 8). Remove the spacer blocks after nailing the center trim.

Glue and nail the sills (H) at the top and bottom edges

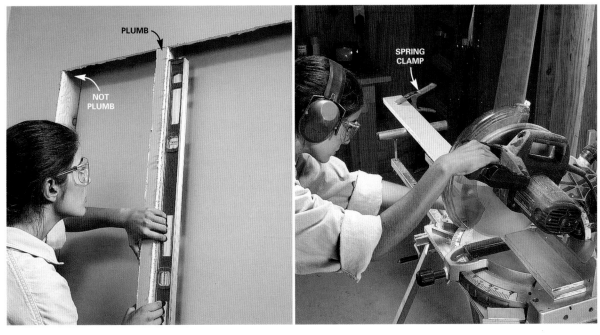

3 Check the studs for plumb and adjust the width and spacing of the boxes as needed in your plan to allow them to slip in easily (Photo 10).

4 Cut out all the pieces, following the dimensions in the Cutting List or your own plan. Clamp and gang-cut matching parts when possible.

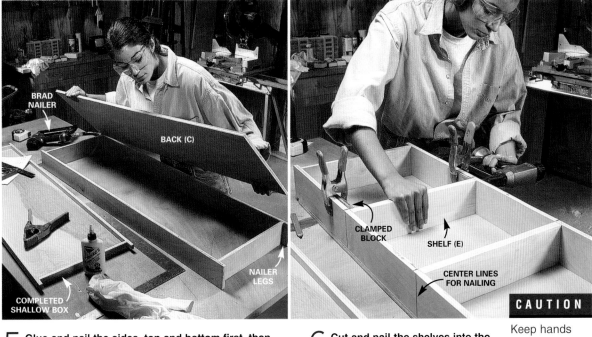

5 Glue and nail the sides, top and bottom first, then glue and nail on the 1/2-in. plywood back (C) to square each box. Wipe off excess glue with a damp rag.

6 Cut and nail the shelves into the deep box. Clamp square blocks to the sides to hold the shelf at a right angle while you nail it.

CAUTION

Keep hands

well away from

the power nailer.

of the boxes (Photo 8). Center them on the center trim. They'll overlap the side trim by about 1/2 inch. Then glue and nail the side trim (G) flush with the edges of the boxes. Nail the sills to the side trim as well with 1-1/2-in. brads. Cut the nailers (D) and nail them to the tops and bottoms of the boxes to support the top and bottom trim (Photo 8). Finally, glue and nail on the crossbars (J); see Photo 9 and Figure A.

Take a break and let the glue set up. Then sand out all the rough edges. Paint it now, rather than waiting until it's up.

Set the message center into the wall

The message center should slide right into the opening that you cut in the wall and cover all the rough edges as well (Photo 10). Level it and adjust the height before nailing it to the studs through the trim with 2-1/2-in. finish nails.

You can install doors after mounting the cabinet in the wall, but it's easier to do it before. Install a door (K) on the upper part of the deep box, and a small, drop-down writing surface (L) below it. Special hinges hold the drop-down door at 90 degrees without supports (photo, at right). These doors are both inset, so they have to be aligned with each other and evenly spaced in relation to the trim. This can take some time and patience. At first, install the hinges with only one screw in the adjustable slot, then lock them into place with additional screws after all adjustments are complete.

Fill and sand all nail holes, then paint the message center if you haven't already done so. Finally, install knobs on the doors and put the message center to use.

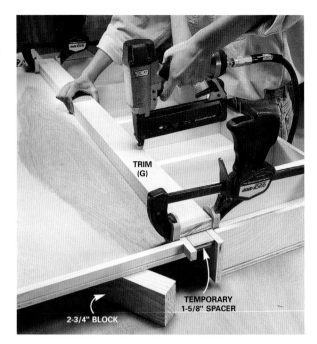

7 Prop the shallow box even with the deeper one, space them with a 1-5/8-in. block and clamp them. Nail on the center trim (G).

TRIM (G)

TEMPORARY 1-5/8" SPACER

2-3/4" BLOCK

Use a no-mortise, partial wrap-around hinge for the upper doors and a self-closing surface-mounted hinge with a 90-degree stop for the drop-down desk. See Resources, p. 186, for suppliers.

UPPER DOOR HINGE

LOWER DOOR HINGE

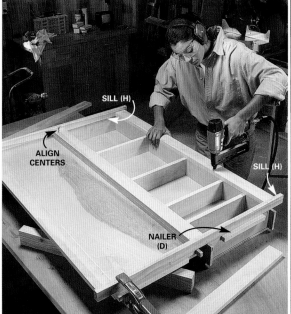

8 Center the top and bottom sills (H) and glue and nail them to the center trim. Glue and nail the side trim (G) to the sides and to the sills. Glue and nail 3/4-in. x 3/4-in. blocks to the top and bottom for nailers (D).

9 Nail on the top and bottom trim (F). Position and clamp the two 1/2-in. x 3/4-in. crossbars (J). Nail with 1-in. brads.

10 Set the completed message center in the opening and level it. Then nail through the trim into the studs to secure it.

11 Screw hinges to the doors and align them in the openings. Inset doors can be fussy to adjust—use just one screw per hinge until you complete the alignment (see Handy Hints®, p. 172).

Stackable shelves

A shop-made jig makes this project simple to build and a snap to assemble

I f you need shelving, storage, a desk or a work surface, check out this modular system. It's got lots of storage space for your electronic gear and books and a nifty recess to accommodate a stool. And you can easily customize this system to suit your storage needs and wall space.

The T-shaped standards (Photo 5) are simple to cut and glue. (Baltic birch was used because of the rich look of the multiple laminations on the edges, but any 1/2-in. hardwood plywood will do.) Sturdy, easy-to-clean 3/4-in. Melamine was used for the horizontal shelves because it has a tough, plasticlike surface, but you can use plywood, MDF (medium-density fiberboard) or particleboard and paint it any color you wish.

The plywood standards and the shelves are drilled precisely with a homemade jig (Photos 4 and 6 and Figure B, p. 179) and are held together with 3/8-in.-dia. steel pins. The pins slide through the shelves and into the standards, so putting this together is sort of like stacking blocks or Lego pieces.

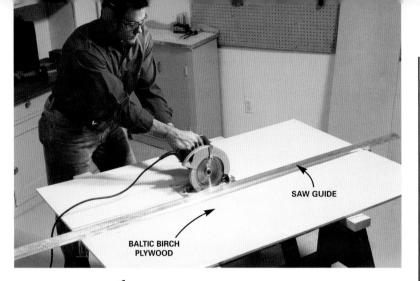

SAW GUIDE

BALTIC BIRCH PLYWOOD

1 Rip your 1/2-in. plywood into pieces to make the standards, then cut the lengths with a circular saw. Cutting large sheets with a straightedge guide and a circular saw is easier than wrestling large sheets through a table saw.

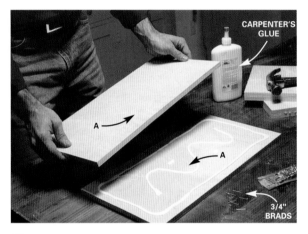

CARPENTER'S GLUE

A

A

3/4" BRADS

2 Glue together the two pieces that make up part A (Figure A, p. 177) of the standards. Nail the two pieces together at two corners with 3/4-in. brads once you've aligned them. This keeps them from drifting apart when you clamp them.

Glue the front pieces together for each standard and then "sandwich clamp" them

It's worth going to the trouble of gluing the 1/2-in. plywood standard fronts together to create a more stable, 1-in.-thick support. This thickness also allows you to use 3/8-in. pins in the assembly for more strength and sturdiness. It would take you a month of Sundays and dozens of clamps to individually clamp all the standard fronts together. Instead, get all your pieces cut and ready to glue and then clamp three or four pairs together at one time as shown in Photo 3.

cutting list

KEY	PCS.	SIZE & DESCRIPTION
A1	6	8" x 18" 1/2" plywood (first-tier standard pieces)
A2	6	9" x 18" 1/2" plywood (second-tier standard pieces)
A3	6	19-3/4" x 18" 1/2" plywood (third-tier standard pieces)
A4	4	16" x 9-1/2" 1/2" plywood (fourth-tier standard pieces)
A5	8	12" x 9-1/2" 1/2" plywood (fifth- and sixth-tier standard pieces)
B1	3	8" x 11-3/4" 1/2" plywood (standard T-end backs)
B2	3	9" x 11-3/4" 1/2" plywood (standard T-end backs)
B3	3	19-3/4" x 11-3/4" 1/2" plywood (standard T-end backs)
B4	2	16" x 11-3/4" 1/2" plywood (standard T-end backs)
B5	4	12" x 11-3/4" 1/2" plywood (standard T-end backs)
C1	6	8" x 5-3/8" 1/2" plywood (standard end blocks)
C2	6	9" x 5-3/8" 1/2" plywood (standard end blocks)
C3	6	19-3/4" x 5-3/8" 1/2" plywood (standard end blocks)
C4	4	16" x 5-3/8" 1/2" plywood (standard end blocks)
C5	8	12" x 5-3/8" 1/2" plywood (standard end blocks)
D1	3	21" x 84" 3/4" Melamine or other sheet good
D2	3	12-1/2" x 44-3/8" 3/4" Melamine or other sheet good
E1	36	3/8" x 2-1/2" steel pins
E2	11	3/8" x 1-1/2" steel pins

figure a
stackable shelves detail

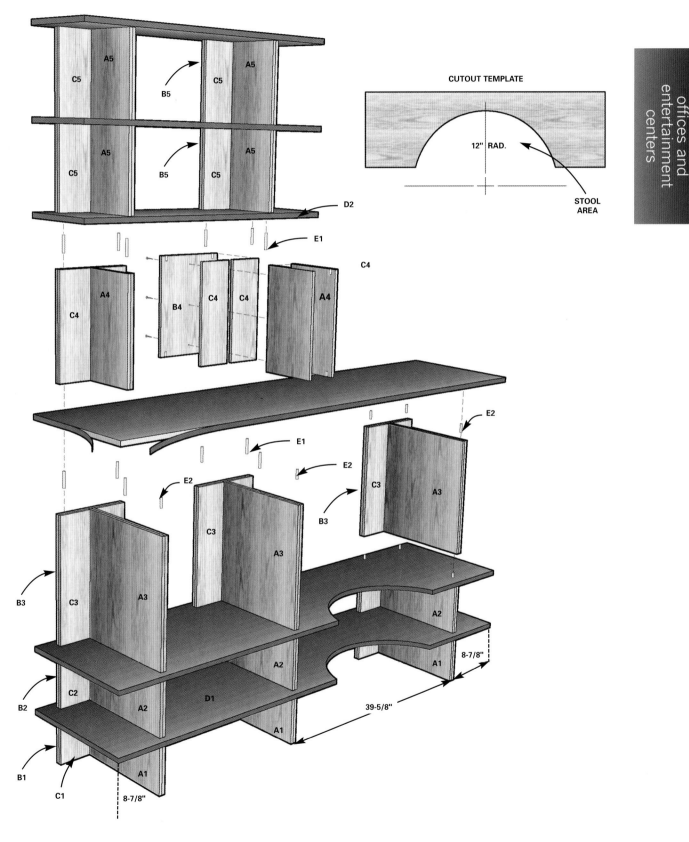

CUTOUT TEMPLATE

12" RAD.

STOOL
AREA

C5 A5 B5 C5 A5

C5 A5 B5 C5 A5

D2

E1

C4 A4 B4 C4 C4 A4 C4

E2

E1

E2

B3 C3 A3 E2 B3 C3 A3

C3 A3 A2

B3 C3 A3 A2

A1

B2 C2 A2 D1

8-7/8"

39-5/8"

8-7/8"

B1 C1 A1

8-7/8"

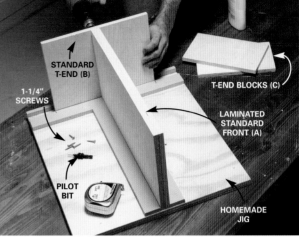

3 Clamp three laminated pairs (A) together using 2x4s to help distribute the pressure evenly across the sheet surface. Leave the assembly clamped for at least two hours.

4 Glue and screw the 1/2-in. plywood back (B) to the laminated part A to form the T-shape of the standard. Be sure to center the standard and make sure everything is aligned. The jig will help with the correct alignment.

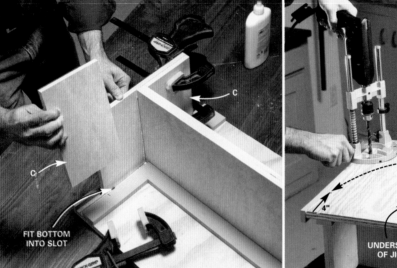

5 Glue and clamp parts C to each standard. Be sure to glue around the perimeter of each piece and also run a bead of glue along the inside corner. Use as many clamps as necessary. For tall standards you may need up to four clamps per side. Remove the standard from the jig and glue another standard together while the glue sets.

6 Drill 25/64-in.-dia. holes 1 in. deep into the tops and bottoms of the standards at the locations shown in Figure B. Here a portable drilling guide (available at home centers) was used for precise perpendicular holes. If you have a good eye for drilling straight holes, you can drill freehand.

Handy Hints®

Cut your Melamine or plywood using a 60-tooth carbide blade in your circular saw. Cut with the good side down to minimize chipping. If you're using black Melamine, you can hide minor chipping with a permanent marker.

7 Cut the assembly pins from 3/8-in. rod using a hacksaw. File the burrs on the cut edge to make the pins easier to slip into the holes.

2-1/2" x 3/8"
DIA. PINS

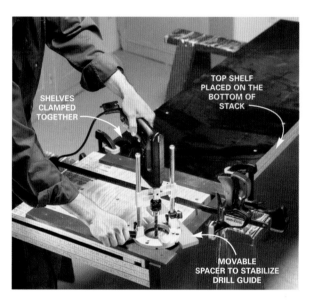

SHELVES CLAMPED TOGETHER

TOP SHELF PLACED ON THE BOTTOM OF STACK

MOVABLE SPACER TO STABILIZE DRILL GUIDE

8 Drill the pin holes in the shelves using the same 25/64-in. drill bit and an accessory fence screwed to the jig. The auxiliary fence positions the jig automatically to ensure consistent overhang from the standards. Be sure to set the depth stop on your drill so you don't drill through the top piece of your shelving unit, which is located on the bottom of the stack as shown.

Measure the height and width you need for each shelf

If you plan to alter this project to suit your personal stuff, establish the height of each shelf so you can cut the plywood for the T-shaped standards. Measure the heights of things you plan to display, like a TV, stereo equipment, computer or books. Also, leave some room from the top shelf to the ceiling.

Build a jig to assemble and drill the T-shaped shelf standards

You can't successfully build this project without maintaining exact consistency. This handy jig will help. You make the jig by gluing and nailing 1/2-in. plywood strips to a 3/4-in. scrap plywood base. Use a square to lay out everything precisely as shown in Figure B. This jig helps you assemble the parts of each standard precisely. And you can flip it over and use it to accurately drill the pin holes (Photo 6).

The jig will also be your guide for drilling the holes into the horizontal shelf boards, which need to perfectly align with the standards (Photo 8). All you need to do is screw an auxiliary fence to the jig to maintain the proper overhang on the front and back of each shelf.

figure b
drilling jig detail

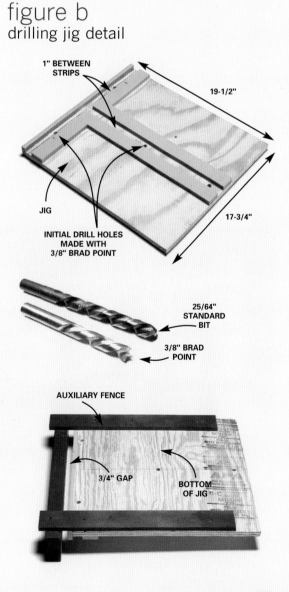

1" BETWEEN STRIPS

19-1/2"

JIG

INITIAL DRILL HOLES MADE WITH 3/8" BRAD POINT

17-3/4"

25/64" STANDARD BIT

3/8" BRAD POINT

AUXILIARY FENCE

3/4" GAP

BOTTOM OF JIG

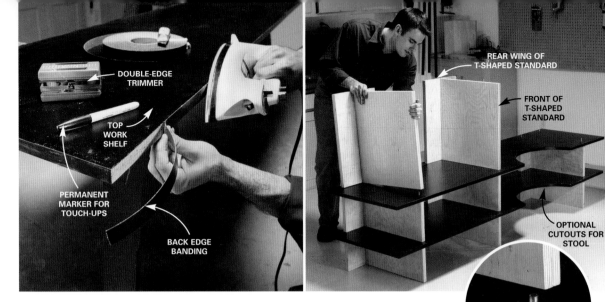

9 Iron the preglued strips onto the edges of the shelves. Use a medium to high setting on the iron. When the glue has set, use a special edge trimmer (available at home centers) for perfect edges. After trimming the edges, sand the edges lightly with 220-grit sandpaper or a fine mill file.

10 Assemble the standards and shelves one tier at a time. Begin by positioning the bottom standards, then align the shelf and tap the pins through the shelf and into the standard.

You don't want your new shelves to sag, so don't exceed a span of 29 in. between the rear wings of the standards. The span is measured from the closest points between the T-shaped standards (Photo 10). For example, if the front edges of your standards are 38 in. apart, the rear wings of the T-shaped standards will be close to 27 in. apart—well within the limit.

Choosing materials

Melamine is a tough material to cut without chipping. If this is one of your first projects, you may want to consider using a different shelf material. In some areas, the black will be difficult to find unless you have a full-service lumberyard special-order it. White Melamine, however, is sold in 3/4-in. thicknesses in most home centers.

Hardwood plywood with iron-on wood edging or MDF (medium-density fiberboard) are excellent substitutes for 3/4-in. Melamine. You can sand the edges of MDF easily, and it paints beautifully because it's so smooth. Plywood is readily available as well, but you'll need either 1/4-in. glue-on strips or iron-on wood edging to cover the exposed edges. You can then stain, varnish or paint the plywood.

Baltic birch may also be tough to find in some areas. It's usually sold in 5-ft.-square sheets. Here nine-ply sheets were used because the cut edges look great when sanded and finished. Each layer, or ply, stands out. And unlike other plywood choices, there are no voids. You can buy Baltic birch with one good side and the other made from lower-quality veneer. This makes the most sense for this project because you can hide the bad side. You can substitute any hardwood plywood, but you may need to glue hardwood strips over the edges to hide voids.

Desktop file holder

A desktop file holder is a great office accessory. It provides easy and immediate access to the files you're currently working with so you don't wear a path between your desk and your file cabinet. This desktop file holder is strong, portable and a snap to make. The only technique that may be new to you is cutting threads with a die. If you've never done this before, it's one of those techniques you'll wonder how you ever got along without. The less adventurous can purchase threaded rods at most home centers.

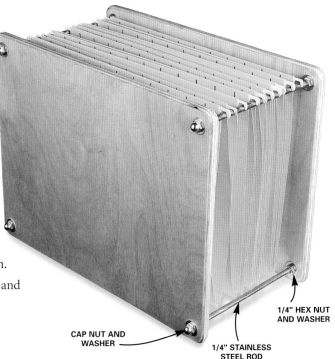

- 1/4" HEX NUT AND WASHER
- CAP NUT AND WASHER
- 1/4" STAINLESS STEEL ROD

- Start by selecting your wood. Shown here is 1/2-in. ApplePly (chosen because it's stable, free of voids and it looks cool with the exposed cap nuts).
- Cut the two 10-1/4-in. by 13-5/8-in. end pieces.
- Lay out and drill the four holes for the steel rod.
- Use a quarter to lay out the corner radius.
- Round over the edges on a router table with a 3/16-in. round-over bit.
- Cut the stainless steel rod (brass works well, too) into 8-in. lengths.

- Cut threads on both ends of the rod with a 1/4-in. die (see photo, below left).
- Sand and finish the sides and assemble.

Use a 1/4-in. die to cut 1-in. threads on each end of the rod. Slightly round the ends of the rod to remove burrs and make it easier to start the die. Keep the die level and use slight downward pressure to start the cut. Once the die begins to cut, it will guide itself. Keep the cutter lubricated with a little light machine oil like 3-In-One.

figure a
plywood layout

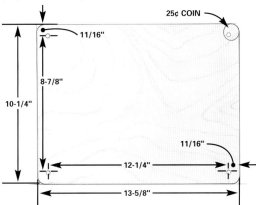

- 25¢ COIN
- 11/16"
- 8-7/8"
- 10-1/4"
- 11/16"
- 12-1/4"
- 13-5/8"

Gallery of ideas

M ainstream cabinet companies offer a wide range of stock, semicustom and custom cabinets that can be arranged and reconfigured in endless ways. Here are some ideas and examples. For more information contact the manufacturers listed in Resources, p. 186.

Photos this page courtesy of Wellborn

A cabinet for everything

Mainline cabinets form the backbone of this home office work area and desk. Crown molding, a bank of cabinet-top drawers, base units containing filing cabinets, laminate tops and custom accessories make this space both attractive and hardworking.

Small and tasteful

Craftsman-style cabinets help turn one corner of this room into a convenient workspace. Filing cabinets built into the lower units provide space for home records and the glass-front upper cabinets help maintain a light, airy feel.

> ## The kitchen-based office
>
> Cabinetry turns the corner and seamlessly incorporates an office area into the space where families naturally congregate—the kitchen. A kneehole drawer suspended between two base drawer cabinets creates the desk; upper cabinets provide plenty of out-of-sight storage.

Photo courtesy of HomeCrest

> ## Behind closed doors
>
> Special full-access, bifold door hardware allows this closet space to be turned into a self-contained office. Standard cabinets, countertop and shelves create the storage and work space.

Photo courtesy of Johnson Hardware

Gallery of ideas

Photo courtesy of Wellborn

Free-standing entertainment center

Furniture-quality cabinets, glass doors and open shelves give this entertainment center a light, airy look. Flipper-style doors, which swing open then hide away along the sides of the center cabinet, provide uninterrupted television viewing from any angle in the room.

The whole room treatment

The raised-panel door style carries through to the paneling, wainscoting and game table. Multiple height base cabinets and an assortment of drawers, bookshelves and closed cabinets create a variety of storage and display options.

Photo courtesy of HomeCrest

Photo courtesy of HomeCrest

Wall-to-wall entertainment

This entertainment center incorporates a fireplace mantle, television cabinet, corner bookshelves, drawers and more. Mid-height cabinets provide display space while allowing windows to be incorporated into the design.

Photo courtesy of KraftMaid

Recessed richness

This tucked-away entertainment center is graced with intricate crown molding, fluted columns and open display shelving. The matching sideboard provides even more storage space for CDs, DVDs and other media equipment.

resource guide

Page 8
Lazy susan hardware available through **Rockler,**
(800) 279-4441,
www.rockler.com

Pages 16-25
Folding L-brackets:
Woodworker's Hardware,
(800) 383-0130,
www.wwhardware.com

Magnetic door catches:
Improvements,
(800) 642-2112,
www.ImprovementsCatalog.com

Page 38
Accuride pantry slides available through **Rockler,**
(800) 279-4441,
www.rockler.com

Page 42
Piano hinges and bottom slides available through **Rockler,**
(800) 279-4441,
www.rockler.com

Page 43
Front moldings manufactured by
House of Fara,
(800) 334-1732,
www.houseoffara.com

Pages 50 & 52
Drawer slides and Titebond Melamine glue available through **Woodworker's Hardware,**
(800) 383-0130,
www.wwhardware.com

Page 57
Epoxy-coated drawer slides available through most hardware stores and home centers.

Page 58
Shelf pins, sleeves and rubber pads available through **Rockler,**
(800) 279-4441,
www.rockler.com

Page 60-61
Photos top and bottom, page 60 and bottom, page 61 by
KraftMaid,
www.kraftmaid.com

Photo top, page 61 by
Plato Woodwork,
www.platowoodwork.com

Page 87
Photo top by
ClosetMaid,
www.closetmaid.com

Photo bottom by
Plato Woodwork,
www.platowoodwork.com

Page 92
Clamp & Tool guide
available through
www.amazon.com
(under "Tools and
Hardware" heading).

Page 106
Kreg pocket screw jig dealer
information:
Kreg Tool Co.,
800-447-8638,
www.kregtool.com

Page 125
Chrome brackets and
rods available through
www.aubuchonhardware.com

Page 126
Keyhole hangers available
through **Woodcraft Supply**
(800) 225-1153,
www.woodcraft.com

Page 150
Rolling stepladders
available through
Putnam Ladder, NY, NY
(212) 226-5147 and
ALACO Ladder, Chino, CA,
(909) 591-7561

Pages 152-153
Complete plans for building
the bookcases shown can be
found in these issues of
The Family Handyman
magazine:

Bookcase and mantel,
Nov 1996, p. 34;

Craftsman-Style Library,
Nov/Dec 1994, p. 42;

Classic Built-in Bookcase,
Dec/Jan 2002, p. 32;

Mission Oak Bookshelves,
Dec/Jan 2003, p. 34.

Back issues are available
through most public libraries.

Pages 156-164
Toggle clamps, TransTint dye,
drawer slides, edge banding and
wood knobs available through
Woodcraft,
(800) 225-1153,
www.woodcraft.com

Page 172
The wrap–around and
self-closing hinges are
available through **Rockler**,
(800) 279-4441,
www.rockler.com

Page 182-185
Photos page 182 and
top 184 from **Wellborn**,
www.wellborn.com

Photo of top 183, bottom of 184
and top of page 185
from **HomeCrest**,
www.homecrestcab.com

Photo bottom of page 183
from **Johnson Hardware**

Photo bottom of page 185,
www.kraftmaid.com

10 Storage Solutions

laundry room helper

If you're remodeling your laundry room, do it with an eye to convenience. Include cabinets with plenty of roll-out wire bins so you can sort clothes by loads—whites, colors, delicates or whatever system you use. Tall cabinets mean less bending over and more counter space for folding and other chores.

Cabinets and bins by HomeCrest Cabinetry. Visit www.homecrestcab.com for more ideas or to find a dealer near you.

can-do storage

You've probably seen those clever inserts for creating storage inside 5-gallon buckets. Now you can do the same with coffee cans. Coffee Can Organizers each have four compartments that nestle neatly inside. A medium-size three-tray set (No. 15061) costs $8.99 plus S&H; a set for large cans (No. 15062) costs $9.99 plus S&H.

Duluth Trading Co., 170 Countryside Dr., P. O. Box 409, Belleville, WI 53508; (800) 505-8888; www.duluthtrading.com.

PHOTO COURTESY OF HOMECREST

3

flip-out sink
front hideaway

If you really want to use every nook and cranny of storage space in your kitchen, consider installing a sink-front tilt tray. This ingenious little device turns even that sliver of wasted space into useful storage, and puts those pot scrubbers and sponges right where you need them—in front of the kitchen sink.

Cabinet with sink tray available through www.kraftmaid.com.

perfect
partners

The "life:stuff:storage" closet system from California Closets offers a wide selection of mix-and-match base and upper storage units that let you customize your closets the way you want. Shown here are the Base Shoe Cubby (left; about $80) and the Top Unit with Hang Rod (right; about $50). Other stacking modules include drawer, open shelf and sliding shelf units. Available in maple and cherry finishes in prices ranging from about $15 to $120.

Available through Target stores; www.target.com.

dream closet

This shoe storage system provides plenty of storage even for the hard-core shoe addict. Wire shelf units mount to wall-mounted tracks in almost limitless configurations.

Available through Lowe's, Home Depot and other retailers. Visit www.closetmaid.com for more design ideas or to find a dealer near you.

stylish high-tech CD storage unit

These multimedia storage cabinets are as hardworking as they are good looking. The doors and drawers of these classic furniture-quality storage units are custom-designed to hold DVDs, CDs and VHS tapes. Choose from a variety of cabinet sizes and finishes.

Available through 27th Avenue; (706) 617-0928, www.27thavenue.com.

super-fast slatwall system

If you've lost track of your workbench top as well as most of your tools, check out the storeWALL. This storage system concept is based on displays that have been used in retail stores for years. Hooks, baskets and storage bins mount securely to the slots in each section; standard 1/4-in. pegboard hooks work as well. The system works great for storing everything from tools to fasteners.

Each plastic section is 15 in. wide and 48 in. long, and available in a variety of colors.
Available through storeWall; www.storewall.com.

shelves in a flash

You can mount one of these to the open studs in your garage or basement quicker than you can say "Stud Buddy." These heavy-duty 18-gauge steel shelves are sturdy enough to support up to 45 lbs., and since they fit between the studs, stuff won't fall off the back. You can choose from a variety of sizes and styles based on your storage needs. Prices start at about $6.

Available directly through Stud Buddy Inc., (888) 578-7452; www.studbuddy.com.

9 handy battery organizer

When the lights go out at your house, do you get tired of playing "Where's the Battery to Fit this Flashlight?" Check out the Battery Rack. It gives you a convenient place to store nearly every size battery, and the tester tells you if a battery is dead, marginal or ready for action. You can mount it on a wall or store it flat in a drawer. The rack (item No. 159139) costs $14.99 plus S&H. The rack with 40 batteries (item No. 210567) costs $69.79 plus S&H.

Available through Improvements Mail Order Catalog; (800) 642-2112; www.improvementscatalog.com.

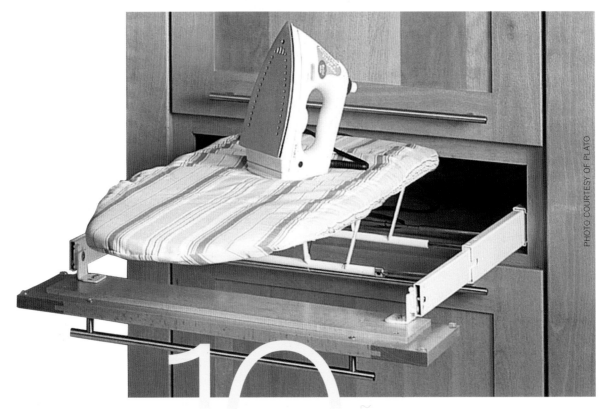

10 pop-out ironing board

You don't have to wrestle with folding, unfolding and figuring out where to put awkward ironing boards each time you do laundry. This in-a-drawer design provides hidden, compact storage for an ironing board—perfect for the laundry room, or even the kitchen, family room or bedroom.

Visit Plato Woodwork at www.platowoodwork.com for more information on cabinets and accessories, or to find a dealer near you.